A FORK IN THE ROAD

Your Guide to a Good Divorce

Gale D. Stanton, MA, OTR/L

TREATY OAK PUBLISHERS

Publisher's Note

A Fork in the Road is a work of individual study and instruction. All of the characters, business establishments, and events are based on the author's personal knowledge and experiences as a licensed occupational therapist and relationship counselor. All quotes and references are shared by permission of each individual or owner.

Copyright © 2017 by Gale D. Stanton, MA, OTR/L
Cover design by Kim Greyer

Printed and published in the United States of America

TREATY OAK PUBLISHERS

ISBN-13: 978-1-943658-22-0
ISBN-10: 1-943658-22-6

DEDICATION

This book is dedicated to anyone who has seriously contemplated divorce or has experienced one.

It is for the vast number of us who consider ourselves failures or losers because we couldn't make good on our promise, "Until death do us part."

For those of us who began with good intentions, yet ended up choosing the wrong mate.

It is a tribute to the brave individuals who left a destructive relationship rather than suffer silently for appearances.

It is dedicated to my exes, my family, friends, teammates, and co-workers who understand the agonizing indecision and shame surrounding divorce.

It is for those who suffered through the self-doubt, pain, and difficult consequences to get to the other side.

TABLE OF CONTENTS

INTRODUCTION

INTRODUCTION

Death is inevitable. Divorce is a choice.

The option to divorce is one reason that makes it is so agonizing. What if you make the wrong decision?

According to the American Psychological Association, 40-50 percent of married couples in the U.S. divorce. The divorce rate is even higher for subsequent marriages.

How one handles the situation can make the difference between personal harmony and hell. Divorce for one partner may be a choice, for the other it may be an unwanted reality. Even couples who recognize their differences as such and decide to split up rarely enter into it equally.

"Cuz when a heart breaks it don't break even." *The Script*

Some insist divorce is not an option. However, unless both partners feel that way, it is always a threat. Divorce doesn't require two consenting parties. It needs only one.

By nature, some relationships are extremely difficult. Doomed from the beginning, the only way to survive them is to leave them. This is especially true when there is repeated verbal or physical abuse. Remaining in a relationship under these circumstances undermines one's confidence and self-esteem. Enduring mistreatment for the sake of the marriage is not only foolish, it can also be dangerous. Long term happiness depends on distancing yourself from the toxic relationship.

Likewise, drug and alcohol abuse are destructive to relationships. They foster an environment where there is excessive worry and preoccupation with the caustic behaviors. Negative interactions and blame become the norm. Remaining in a codependent relationship consumes large amounts of emotional and physical energy from both parties. Being caught up in the dysfunction creates a downward spiral where couples become reactive to each other's bad behavior. This tailspin is difficult to pull out of, especially if the abuser refuses to acknowledge the abuse.

Divorce may be necessary for the preservation of all individuals concerned. When the status quo is no longer acceptable and the strain of the relationship no longer tolerable, it's time for a change. Years of mistreatment chips away at the foundation of any relationship, causing it to crumble under the pressure. However, many couples choose to endure rather than to leave believing that, "Bad breath is better than no breath at all."

When a negative relationship compromises the wellbeing of those involved, a divorce may be the best option. The choice to end the relationship doesn't have to mean the ultimate destruction of the individuals involved. Gwyneth Paltrow describes it as a "conscious uncoupling."

Along those lines, there is a relatively new phenomenon of couples taking selfies at court with their divorce decree in hand. What seems peculiar to outsiders may be evidence of a shift in attitudes regarding how to get divorced as well as divorce itself.

In the past, divorce has been associated with ugly accusations, private detectives, fault finding associates, and battling attorneys. Divorce has the reputation of being messy, painful, costly, and unpleasant. Though divorce is an ugly word, it doesn't have to be an ugly experience. That is not to suggest it won't be painful. However, with the emerging new consciousness, it can be manageable, enlightening, and fair. The two people involved in the split have the opportunity to create their own truth. A good divorce.

At some point in most relationships, one partner or both come to a fork in the road. There is a deliberate effort made to stay the course of the relationship or deviate from the path. The off-roading committed by partners can be emotional, physical, or both. It consists of the desire to drive away and leave your partner in the dust. The urge can be so strong that the consequences of such an action are trivialized or overlooked. Traveling to an unknown destination is particularly alluring when you are dissatisfied with your current location.

In order to navigate this juncture successfully, one must develop a formula and be careful not to follow a fantasy. All couples fantasize what it would be like to have the perfect relationship. This is helpful when projecting where you want the relationship to go because it points you in the right direction. However, perfect is not viable. Leaving a good relationship in search for a flawless one is irrational.

The answer to the question whether divorce is the best option requires insight and investigation. Understanding the state of affairs and what went wrong without blaming your partner is key. You are fifty percent of the equation, even if your spouse is an abuser, an infidel, or a monster. You subjected yourself to being involved with this person and your question should be, "Why?"

The road to happiness requires looking within. Comprehending what went wrong in basic terms is essential. Attempting to fix problems and resolve issues will alleviate guilt later on with respect to not having given it your all. Realizing when enough is enough takes time and effort. After much soul searching, research, and analysis, the decision to end the relationship must include preparing for what happens next.

Divorce is a death of sorts. Partners go through the grieving process and develop a new way of moving forward. *A Fork in the Road* acts as a guide to determine if divorce is the best option for you. Is it something you desire to do and if so, why? Are you equipped to handle the roadblocks and setbacks along the way? Are you fully aware of the pain, the pitfalls, and the decrease in lifestyle?

A Fork in the Road navigates every aspect of divorce and provides strategies on how to do it with knowledge, deliberation, and love. The goal is to minimize the hurt, diminish the long-term negative consequences, and speed up the recovery time. You may not have wanted to get a divorce; however, when you find yourself in the middle of one, as people often do, you can learn how to make it a good one.

SECTION ONE

Stop. Assess Where You Are.

SECTION ONE

Stop. Assess Where You Are.

How did you come to the fork in the road? Where have you previously journeyed and where do you want to go?

A road map highlighting your relationship route is helpful at this point. It pinpoints your current location and where you navigated prior. It illustrates your passage by providing an overview of where you began, how you got lost, and where you need to go.

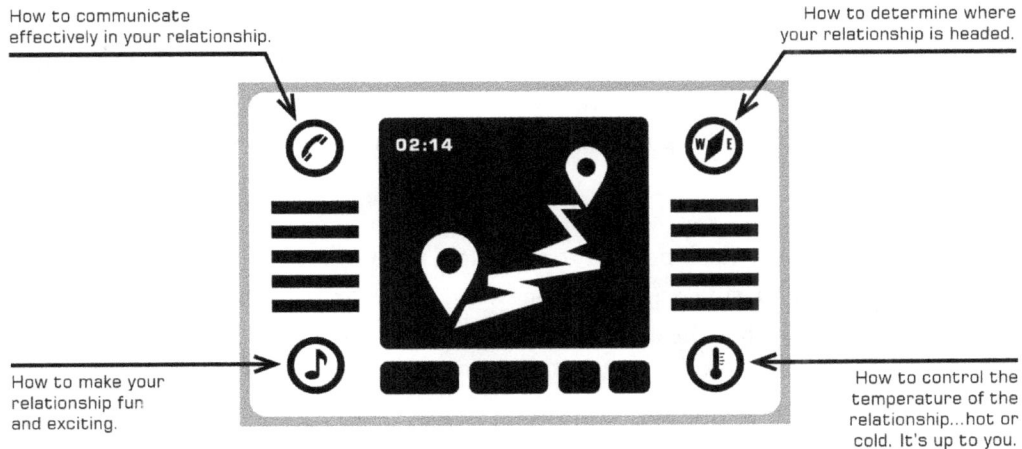

How to communicate effectively in your relationship.

How to determine where your relationship is headed.

How to make your relationship fun and exciting.

How to control the temperature of the relationship...hot or cold. It's up to you.

The problem is that relationships, unlike modern vehicles, do not have navigational systems built into them. Also, the map for a successful partnership is not universal or one-size fits-all. Relationships are as unique as snowflakes. Though certain core principles are inherent in all fulfilling relationships, the map for any long term partnership is developed by the two individuals in it. Most couples do not chart out their course. They hope for the best and let it unfold.

You can't build a house, car, or relationship without a blueprint. The necessary components of a relationship are similar to the parts of a car. If one or several are missing, it won't function properly. It's impossible to wind up in the same place as your partner without some strategic planning. It isn't surprising that couples find themselves drifting apart and going off course when they seek different destinations. Without a a well thought out template that both partners agree upon, individuals wander aimlessly attempting to meet their individual needs along with their partner's expectations. If those two things are incompatible, the trouble begins.

Let's assume the navigational system is down and the blueprint absent when one partner encounters a fork in the road. It's confusing to be lost and not know where to turn. The first thing that should take place is to pull over, stop the car, and assess the situation.

This is easier said than done. Proper calculation of where to go next requires self-awareness. Evaluating the situation with precision necessitates tabling your emotions and possessing the ability to see things from your partner's point of view.

ASSESS, PAUSE, AND REFLECT. Is the desire to travel into unknown territory a reflection of the relationship or of you personally? It is absolutely essential to examine the origin of your restless urge to run. You are in the driver's seat and this is your trip. When you realize you aren't where you want to be, first analyze who you are.

Is your current location a choice you made, or do you feel you were coerced into it? I have heard from too many people that they got married due to external pressures, such as society, parents and family, or even their partner's demands. If they hadn't felt the external forces weighing so heavily on them, they would have waited.

Name a person who was most influential in your decision to get married.

_____

The purpose of this exercise is not to assign blame. You ultimately made the choice to marry; however, it helps to understand your motivations at the time. Far too many people say they knew it was a mistake the minute they walked down the aisle. These same individuals claim they shouldn't have had children with their partner, realizing it only after their first child was born. When the second child came along, they resigned themselves to endure for the sake of the family until they couldn't fake it to make it any longer.

Are you feeling a sense of general discontent or can you identify exactly what troubles you? Is it an overall sense of helplessness or more specific, such as your job, geographical location, living conditions, money, spouse, or children?

List two major things that disappoint you today.

_____

_____

Happiness is an inside job. If my happiness is dependent on you, then I am not developed as a person. It is my responsibility to live life in a manner that makes me happy, and it is up to me to discover exactly what that means. Couples should complement one another, not depend on their partners to make them happy.

How long have you felt your life was not on track? Has it been six days or six years? Can you identify the 'aha moment' or epiphany when you felt you or your relationship derailed?

If so, list it below.

_____

_____

Statistics have shown it takes couples an average of seven years of discontent before they seek marital counseling. By then it is often too late. They have allowed their relationship to deteriorate to a point where ending it would be easier than mending it. Bad habits have become repetitive and the desire to modify them has diminished. Not talking about one's day or not going to bed together at night has become routine.

Without blaming your spouse or your parents, how you have contributed to losing your way? Did you have access to a map and ignored it or did you hope fate would lead you down the right path?

List two things you would do differently if given a chance.

_____

_____

The fundamental truth here is ownership. It's easier to fault your partner than to discover your contribution to the problem. This process may require a third party to help you see things more clearly, or it may require time and space to gain perspective.

It wasn't until after my divorce that I saw how my financial expectations, social demands, and capricious nature created problems for my husband. He was fiscally conservative, introverted, and not a risk taker. My personality contributed to his feelings of discomfort. Never feeling he was enough, he shut down emotionally.

Are you one to get going when the going gets tough or do you prefer to take the path of least resistance? Do you follow through with projects or are you one to give up and move on to something else? Are you more determined than most or do you go with the flow to make peace?

List two major endeavors you saw to conclusion. List two you quit before completion. Were they good decisions for the most part or do you have regrets?

Completed:

_____

_____

Abandoned:

_____

_____

It is important to observe your patterns and determine those that have served you as well as those that have hurt you. Many women stay in relationships too long. Risking their emotional wellbeing, they take on the role of the enabler. Threatening their personal safety, they attempt to understand their abuser. Jeopardizing their self-esteem, they remain married to a serial cheater. Whatever pattern you uncover, decide if it is something you wish to continue.

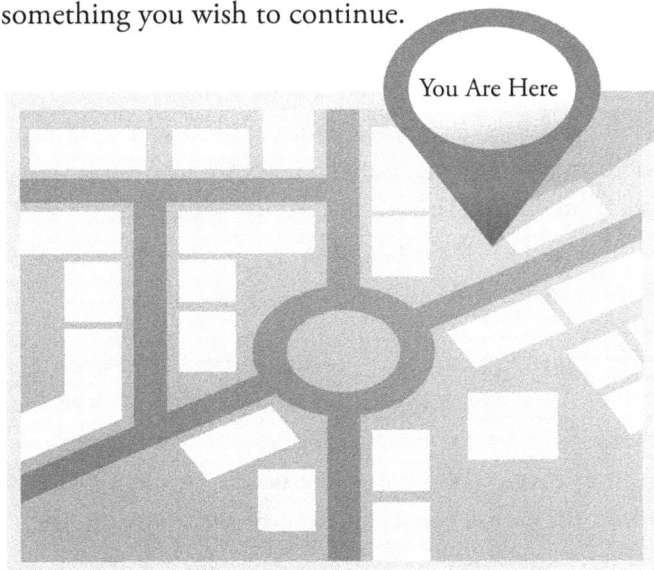

ASSESS YOUR INDIVIDUAL STRENGTHS AND WEAKNESSES. Are you enterprising or do you prefer safety and security over the stressful unknown? How well do you know your personal preferences?

Some questions you should ask yourself are these:

- Are you more spontaneous or schedule driven?

- Do you embrace change or does it stress you out?

- Do you feel the need always to be in charge or can you let someone else lead?

- Are you adventurous or more conservative?

- Do you prefer routine or variation?

- Do you live near your extended family or did you move away for opportunity?

- Are you well-traveled or more of a home body?

- Are you flexible and roll with the punches or more rigid and unyielding?

- Do you look forward with anticipation or backward with regret?

- Do you have a glass half empty or a glass half full outlook?

Divorce requires courage, stamina, and the ability to embrace whatever the future holds. There may be several setbacks before any successes. As difficult as it is, it should be approached with a fair amount of positivity and optimism. By evaluating your emotional fitness, you can better determine if the risk of leaving the relationship is worth the reward.

Due to the fact that the road and destination are undecided, fear and doubt often cause the individuals divorcing to act irrationally. Couples blame each other for the failed relationship, as opposed to looking within, and seek allies who will back them up in their denial. Bitterness and battles result. Divorce is difficult and for some not worth the consequences. Are you prepared for the challenges that terminating your marriage requires?

ASSESS THE CONSEQUENCES OF DRIVING AWAY ON A SEPARATE PATH. Are you willing to lose it all? Home, money, family support, time with children and pets. It is much harder than it looks. You may choose to leave a situation that appears insufferable only to experience unbearable loneliness and isolation. Whether you stay in the relationship or end it, you need to delineate the financial and emotional costs.

I have known several men who express ongoing discontent in their marriage. They profess to want out, yet remain year after year. Some say things like, "It's cheaper to keep her," or "I don't really love her anymore, but it's about the kids."

I have counseled individuals who premeditated their departure for as long as ten years. Within months of the youngest child graduating from high school, they filed for divorce. Statistics show that 80% of women file for the divorce, leaving only 20% of men initiating it. Many men will criticize yet endure an unhappy marriage so as not to be separated from their children or deal with the financial burden of dividing assets and paying child support. Better at compartmentalizing their marriage into one aspect of their lives, men prefer to cope with the situation rather than dissolve it, whereas women have difficulty separating their marital relationship from all other aspects of their lives, leaving them miserable most of the time.

ASSESS HOW BAD THE SITUATION FEELS TO YOU. Your perception is your reality. Others may see you and your partner as having a great relationship; however, only you know how it really functions. Sometimes things feel intolerable when in reality it just isn't ideal. Perfect relationships don't exist because perfect people don't exist. There is no unicorn out there. By unicorn I am referring to that perfect image of a partner you create in your mind. Understand the difference between reality and fantasy. Regarding the crossroads you find yourself at currently, consider the following:

Is it acute or chronic?

Are the disagreements between you and your partner infrequent yet explosive, or do they appear to be a constant drain on your relationship? Some couples describe their relationship as love/hate. When they are in agreement, they are in love. All is fabulous until controversy arises and causes tempers to flare. Once ignited, the fuse is difficult to extinguish, resulting in a fight. This acute disharmony may be a simple fix, such as learning how to fight fair or knowing when to pick your battles.

Other couples describe their problem as an underlying hostility and resentment that erodes the foundation of their love on a consistent basis. They describe walking around each other at home, avoiding contact or interaction. Cohabitating in silence, they are not a team as much as they are two individuals occupying the same residence. A solution for this type of chronic tension is not so easy and may require in-depth therapy, separation, or divorce.

MILEAGE

| 5 | 7 | 4 | 3 |

Is it time sensitive?

Over the course of a long term relationship, life events transpire. The death of a parent, the birth of a child, loss of a job, relocation, etc. These stressors impact our intimate relationships greatly. They may result in situational depression, fear, panic, and a low tolerance for dealing with your partner.

Sometimes intervention is needed for couples to get them over the bumps in the road until they adjust to the life event that is causing them to react negatively to each other. We tend to blame the relationship for our absence of pleasure, when it is a momentary problem that will be remedied or adjusted to with time.

How many days of the week or month do you experience angst over your relationship?

Record the days you are unhappy with your partner. Individuals tend to remember traumatic events and forget the good times in between. You may perceive your disagreements to be happening all the time, when in actuality they may erupt once or twice a month. Tracking and monitoring them will create a baseline. This baseline will minimize the emotions associated with the conflict and reveal the facts.

Along with monitoring the number of fights, jot down the trigger events that cause them. Examples would include rude or insensitive comments, acting selfishly or being inconsiderate, ignoring or disregarding your feelings, belittling you, etc. This will help you discover the recurring problems as well as their frequency.

CALENDAR

Sunday	Monday	Tuesday	Wednesday	Thursday	Friday	Saturday

Have the problems in your relationship bled into other areas of your life? Has it interfered with your job, friendships, or family?

Are you unable to focus at work because of a preoccupation about your relationship? Are you quick to anger with co-workers, family, or friends as a direct result of the difficulties in your marriage? Do you avoid family gatherings or associating with friends because you fear a fight will ensue with your partner?

If your relationship is disrupting other aspects of your life, you need to get to the root of the problem before the damage is compounded. Manage it before it gets to the tipping point that leaves you in the path of destruction.

If you have children, are they experiencing negative effects from the conflict with your partner?

The fallout from fighting, arguing, or silent hostility impacts day to day interactions and your children's wellbeing. I've counseled couples who admit to witnessing their children putting their hands over their ears to block out the shouting or heated discussions. Equally as damaging are the spouses who avoid each other with limited conversation and silent hostility. Children perceive the emotions and subtle vibrations of those around them. Whether the discord comes in the form of a loud backfire or silent misfire, children are in tune with their surroundings.

For the most part, therapists agree that children from a negative, dysfunctional household tend to do worse than those living in a divided one. Dual households come with pluses and minuses depending on how parents handle the situation. Children of divorce often admit it was the best thing their parents did, even though it was painful and frightening at the time. Children reflect the attitudes of their parents. Peace can follow a split if all parties are willing to compromise and work at it. Too many times the kids are used as pawns rather than protected from the repercussions of the divorce.

Have you found yourself attempting to sabotage your relationship by engaging in addictive behaviors? Drinking, gambling, overeating, shopping, avoidance, or seeking attention from outsiders?

These addictive behaviors may be result of a personality disorder or they may be unhealthy coping mechanisms. They could be used to momentarily escape from an undesirable relationship or they may be a cry for help. Acting out in this way is usually a symptom of a bigger problem. Individuals who are chronically unhappy and feel hopeless in a relationship often sabotage it. Too paralyzed to fix it or end it, they engage in risk-taking behaviors until they hit bottom. Fear of confronting the problem head on or lacking the ability to communicate their inner feelings, they draw attention to it by doing something counterproductive.

This challenge to the balance in the relationship forces the partners to deal with their unsatisfactory marriage. Once at the crossroads, couples must decide on a new direction. Together or apart.

ASSESS WHERE TO GO FROM HERE.

Turn the car around. Go back home. Now that you have determined that your relationship is in trouble and that you cannot continue driving in that direction, stop and take a step back. It is imperative that you set out to establish whether your relationship issues are simply navigating bumps in the road, or if they are more serious and long-lasting.

Your relationship may require a complete engine overhaul or perhaps it has already crashed and burned. Figure out where you are and where you need to go.

Go back to the basics.

I suggest you read ***Two For The Road – A Relationship Manual Designed for Him and Essential for Her***. It is an easy to read handbook for couples that covers the fundamentals of relationships from beginning to end. It provides an overview of how to have a successful marriage and is a great place to start. It also includes other resources to assist with getting your relationship headed in the right direction.

Review the timeline of your relationship – the maintenance schedule, if you will.

Where have you two journeyed and how did you get to where you are now? What did the joyrides look like and when did they stop? When did you first notice signs of trouble? What contributed to the two of you driving off in different directions?

Diagnose the problem.

Though there may be several issues as it is rarely just one thing, it is a necessary to define the most damaging aspects of your relationship. Lack of intimacy, teamwork, self-discipline, honesty, money etc. Or too much time apart, conflict, craziness, etc. Whether it is not enough of something, too much of another, or both, these discoveries must take place. Either to get the marriage back on track or to recognize the futility of such an option. Become informed partners to understand what drove you to this point.

Who is to blame?

The answer to that question is you BOTH are to blame. Know thyself. Does your discontent have more to do with you, your choice in partners, or life in general? Where you stand on this is where you look. In all cases, it begins and ends with you. Perhaps it's a wound you need to heal regarding your past, or maybe you need to learn to handle life's stressors better. Any way you slice it, if you are a bad driver, a new car won't help.

Where do you want to go?

This is your map. Do you feel you have done all that you can do? Are you at the end or the beginning? Change is possible, it's just not easy. Unfortunately, rarely are couples synchronized in this effort. In most cases, one partner has already checked out and is waiting for the right opportunity to leave the relationship.

When is divorce the best option?

When you have completed all the research, soul searching, and homework necessary to understand the problem and feel you have done all you can do. There is another option. The good divorce. Though it sounds like an oxymoron, it is possible. Labeled by some as a conscious uncoupling, it is a split that doesn't carry all of the undesirable connotations and stereotypical overtones that have been associated with divorce in the past. Once you admit you both would be better off without the other and the relationship has become toxic, it is time to move on.

Divorce is never the original goal.

No one enters into marriage with the expectation they will split up, however, it has become a definite reality. Divorce, like it or not, deserves deliberate consideration. The opportunity to have a good divorce or an amicable split is possible. It requires a great deal of self-restraint, maturity, self-awareness, and perspective taking. Letting go of the bitterness and egocentric behaviors is essential. A good divorce involves education, patience, understanding, and love of the greater good.

SECTION TWO

How Did You Get Here?

SECTION TWO

How Did You Get Here?

Whether you decide the relationship is fixable or doomed, it is important to understand the roadblocks and detours that contributed to the difficulties in the relationship. Defining what went wrong and how you both lost your way is not only important for your current relationship; it is critical for any relationship going forward. How did you end up where you are now?

Where did you make a wrong turn? What caused the relationship to derail? Did you zone out and, by the time you realized it, you had difficulty finding your way home? Were you driving too fast in the wrong direction, hoping to escape? Did you not perform maintenance and tune ups on yourself, the relationship, or the road? There are numerous reasons couples experience trouble in their relationship from lack of intimacy to constant conflict. Write down the top three issues you believe are damaging your relationship:

_____

_____

_____

Most will discover they fall into one of five major categories: Too much conflict, lack of intimacy or sex, absence of trust, loss of respect, lack of common ground. Without being too much of a reductionist, most issues are related in one form or another to one of these five groupings.

WE FIGHT ALL THE TIME AND CAN'T GET ALONG ANYMORE.

Conflict comes in many forms for many reasons. Disagreements may result in heated arguments or silent hostility. Explosive debates could last for a couple hours or develop into the silent treatment for weeks. Whatever pattern of conflict you develop as a couple, there are ways to diminish the perpetual struggle. There is no such thing as a relationship without some discord, so don't expect it. Instead, seek ways to better handle conflict when it arises.

Corrosive elements leave permanent damage whether we are discussing automobiles or relationships. Constant disagreement erodes the foundation of relationships. In order to protect our relationship from these toxic effects, we need to determine how to handle problems or avoid them when possible.

Disparity is inevitable between partners. Differing realities contribute to opposing points of view. Where the opposite sex is concerned, biology influences how each individual sees things, as well as how they react to them. Men and women possess unique differences and that's okay. Men tend to be more logical, linear thinkers and women are reported to be emotional connectors. One can argue this came from the hunter/gatherer model of our ancestors and we have evolved to more of a unisex existence.

Though that may be true with more women taking on career responsibilities and an increase of stay-at-home dads, the male/female divide remains. Understanding and respecting the gender based qualities of one another is necessary for conflict resolution and a more harmonious relationship.

Gender differences are not the only road blocks that create conflict. Personality preferences should be considered as well. Opposites attract initially but can they go the distance? Are extroverts better with extroverts and introverts with introverts?

According to the MEYERS-BRIGGS TYPE INDICATOR, preferences influence the way we interact with each other as well as the world. These preferences affect our love lives, career choices, and our life satisfaction in general. They are listed as extraversion vs. introversion, sensing vs. intuition, thinking vs. feeling, and judging vs. perceiving. Depending where you are on the scale, predictions can be made about how you handle certain situations.

After we were married, my ex-husband and I discovered we were opposite in every category. What once was exciting in the beginning became an arduous effort in the end. He possessed many qualities I respected and felt deficient in overall. In that way, one could say he completed me, providing what I lacked. However, in the end our differences created constant dissention in our lives. Though we were able to understand our dissimilarities, we couldn't overcome the problems they created in our marriage. Both of us moved on to marry partners who were more similar to us.

Another source of conflict I mention in my book, **Two For The Road**, is a difference in upbringings. How we were raised, as a member of a large family or as an only child, created our individual realities. Our parents were our role models on how to behave as a partner. Whether we followed their example or grew up determined not to repeat their mistakes, we observed their relationship and were influenced by it.

We were also swayed by our family values, habits, food preferences, and more. Though siblings may vary in personalities, their experiences as a unit shaped them. How they spent the holidays, attitudes about private school and formal education, spending habits, political views, etc., can be traced back to family environments. These can also be sources of debate. When one partner insists on doing it their way because that's just how it is done, consideration and compromise are required to avoid conflict.

Couples need to be equally invested in managing the relationship. If one partner does all the work and the other is absent, conflict is sure to follow. Two people should desire to work on their relationship together. Sharing the responsibility for the good and the bad aspects of their marriage strengthens the concept of being a team. It also emphasizes individual culpability. A unilateral approach by either partner is destructive in nature. One-sided decisions or secretive motives are counterproductive to relationships.

Effective partners confront what causes them distress and explore how to diminish or resolve it. Both should have a desire to understand each other, appreciating their partner for the interesting and unique person that they are.

One significant element necessary in handling differences is trying to understand your partner's point of view. This does not mean you must agree with their POV, but an attempt to see where they are coming from will provide insight. Replace blame with empathy. Acknowledge your partner's issues without judgment. Eliminate the black and white thinking that prevents you from being able to resolve the struggle.

When clashing with your partner, don't think of it as a competition. No one person has to win while the other loses. Eradicate right and wrong absolutes. Eliminate the need to be right at all costs. Consider that your relationship is a cooperative effort. It's about collaboration and mutual responsibility. Joint harmony can take you and your partner a greater distance than the personal satisfaction of being right. Proving your partner wrong does little to unite your efforts. It has the opposite effect. There are times when it isn't worth the fight.

Listen more and talk less. We have two ears and one mouth. There is a difference between hearing and listening. Active listening requires us to avoid getting defensive. If we are thinking about how to respond, then we aren't fully present. Listening includes being attentive to both the verbal and nonverbal expressions from our partner. Not only do we need to focus on what is being said, we also must consider and observe what isn't being said.

Ideally we should encourage our partner to express their thoughts and feelings in a nonthreatening way. This is impossible to achieve when emotions are high. The best thing to do in the heat of the moment is to pause, walk away, and take a time out until tempers have calmed. Then return with the intention to listen in order to understand.

Owning your contribution to the disharmony in the relationship is vital. This not only confirms what you need to work on as an individual, but it also helps to break down the barrier so your partner can admit their participation in the problem. Accountability is instrumental in any relationship. Own up to your responsibility to know and to grow. You can't develop as a person or a partner until you acknowledge your shortcomings and the negative impact they have on your relationship. We all bring our stuff into the relationship, good and bad. Discerning what serves you and what doesn't is essential to your evolution as a suitable mate.

When all else fails, escape the situation until cooler heads prevail. Take a walk, a drive, or go workout. When reason, respect, and rationality fall by the wayside, STOP. Take yourself out of the conflict that has escalated to the point where nothing good can come from it. Attempting to calm either partner is futile and will only end poorly. Exclamations such as, "I can't stand you," or "I want a divorce," are likely to be spewed in anger. When discussions have turned into tirades that include temper tantrums and acting out, leave the situation. This is a time to walk, not talk. Write, not fight.

Writing a letter to your partner about how you feel does a number of positive things. It allows you to center yourself, sort through your emotions, organize your thoughts, and choose your words wisely. Being in this frame of mind helps distance you from the conflict in order to see it more clearly.

When you remove yourself from an argument that has become destructive, you put yourself into a productive place where the healing can begin. Writing permits you to express yourself freely without immediate backlash from your partner. It creates an opportunity for your partner to read and process your words without interruption. The written word helps your partner to process your thoughts in a non-threatening environment at their pace and in their own way.

WARNING: *This only works if the words are not accusatory or angry. A clear and calm head must prevail. It will backfire if you engage in name calling or verbal abuse.*

⚠ WARNING

This symbol means there is something that could hurt you or other people.

With conflict inherent in every relationship, avoiding it by not acknowledging the issues is a mistake. By not being mindful and aware, this results in the slow death of the marriage. We often hear about the "perfect couple who never fought" ending up in divorce court. They either concealed their unresolved conflicts or never dealt with them in the first place. The ultimate is to transform conflict into growth. Last but not least, fighting fair when conflicts emerge helps couples to cope.

Fighting fair is everything it implies. There is no exploiting your partner's weaknesses. One of the most damaging things you can do in any relationship is to use trusted information against your partner. Any intimacies they have shared with you are off the table, unless you never want your partner to open up and confide in you again.

Your partner needs to know their vulnerabilities are in your safe keeping. Using them in a fight not only harms the relationship, it also causes your partner to lose respect for you. It undermines their trust in you as a spouse, friend, and confidant.

The obvious motive in using sensitive information against your partner is to hurt them as you have been hurt. However, the damage to the relationship is far worse and longer lasting than any momentary satisfaction you feel in the immediacy of your fight. Chances are they have been dealing with their wound for quite some time and your pouring salt into it only makes you the bad guy.

Some couples utilize a safe word when they feel a disagreement or negative situation is about to take place. It can be any word you both agree on and should be a word others won't recognize as such. The safe word is used to diffuse an argument immediately with no further discussion. It is a signal or cue to your partner that you both need to take a step back, get emotions in check, and deal with it at a more appropriate time. One that is not in public, or after a couple glasses of wine, and certainly not in front of the children.

The safe word often coincides with a necessary time-out. Taking a time-out to collect oneself is often the best solution. Whether the reason is to avoid allowing the argument to escalate, to gather one's thoughts, or even to put things in perspective, time-outs are extremely effective.

Conflict doesn't always have to take center stage and be dealt with at that exact moment. Rather than insist it be resolved instantly, take a break until it can be managed at a more advantageous time. Patience is the practice here. The temporary time out isn't intended to ignore or dismiss the problem, it just defers it until there is a better time to address it.

A good tool to have in your toolbox is the ability to recognize when you are wrong and apologize. The apology may not resolve the problem; however, it is a good place to start. In order for apologies to be effective, they must be sincere. A heartfelt expression of regret shows strength, ownership, and concern. The capacity to know when you have gone too far or have unnecessarily hurt someone you love is highly attractive.

By the same token, don't expect or demand an apology in return. Though you may deserve one, asking for one is like asking for a compliment. It doesn't mean anything unless your partner offers it freely and unsolicited.

I LOVE MY PARTNER BUT I AM NO LONGER "IN LOVE" WITH THEM.

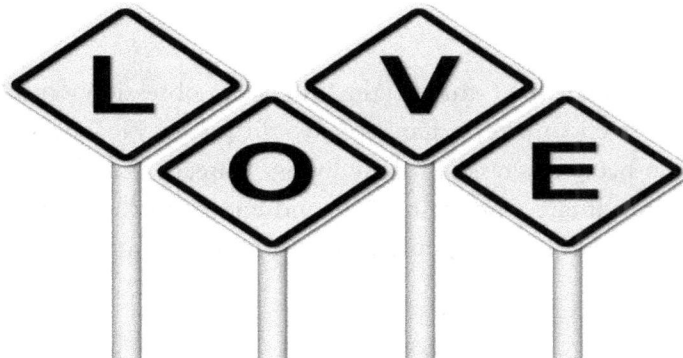

Long term relationships become routine after a while. Just as conflict is inherent in relationships, so is the fact that relationships mature. The hot and heavy excitement of infatuation has been reported to dissipate between eighteen months and two years. The three-times-a-day sex becomes three times a week and may eventually develop into three times a month. Women's magazines are loaded with articles targeted toward keeping the love alive.

My father used to say, "Familiarity breeds contempt." The saying is old, but the message is timeless. Knowing someone inside and out so well that you can predict their behavior with great accuracy can become tedious and in some cases annoying.

There is nothing sexy about being compared to a comfortable old shoe. Couples constantly strive for balance between the intensity and novelty of new love and the cozy and secure nature of a long term relationship. (Simpson, Campbell, and Berscheid, psychologyinspain.com, 2011) described the difference between romantic or passionate love and affectionate or companionate love. Passionate love or "eros" is often seen in the early part of a love relationship and consists of strong sexual and infatuation components. This is often referred to as being "in love" with someone.

Their studies show, "More than half of the people today say that not being 'in love' is sufficient reason to get a divorce." This is staggering, considering that long term infatuation is not sustainable. (Simpson, Campbell and Berscheid, 1986)

Affectionate love is when individuals desire to be near to each other and express a deep caring adoration for their partner. Social scientists believe the early stages of love have more romantic components, but as love matures, passion gives way to affection.

I've heard it explained that if the intensity, obsession, and preoccupation of infatuation lasted forever, exhaustion would set in. No one would be able to accomplish the necessary tasks of daily living. Careers and children would suffer, as it takes an inordinate amount of time and energy in the early stages of love to maintain it. The focus needs to shift at some point to establishing more balance in life.

Couples need to determine if their expectations regarding the relationship and their feelings for each other are too high. Did they expect the honeymoon would never end? Did they presume the excitement of their relationship should remain as intense as it was in the beginning? When reality set in and the infatuation stage ended, did they find themselves bored or disappointed? Did familiarity kill the romance? Did they discover deficiencies in each other that were overlooked in the throes of passion? Has routine and monotony become the norm?

Boredom is a self-imposed problem. If you are bored, it is your fault. It is not up to your partner or anyone else to entertain you. Self-fulfillment, like happiness, is your job, not someone else's. If you find your relationship has gone stale, look within.

Dissatisfaction and boredom may cause you to consider whether you chose the wrong partner. However, you should examine whether that feeling is an internal or external issue. Internal meaning that you may have a general dissatisfaction or malaise toward life in general. External might mean your partner got lazy and stopped trying. Take a personal inventory first before leaving the relationship and placing the blame on your partner.

Understand the difference between infatuation and enduring love. There are numerous reports that suggest there is a chemical reaction that occurs in the brain when we experience infatuation. It is described as a high which is created from the release of natural endorphins. Endorphins such a norepinephrine and dopamine trigger a positive feeling in our bodies similar to amphetamines. When this intense chemical reaction ceases to exist with our long-term partner, we may confuse the lack of euphoria with falling out of love with them.

Psychologist Robert J. Sternberg's triangular theory of love describes the fullest type of love to include all three components of passion, intimacy, and commitment. He labeled this as consummate love. These components may not be present in equal amounts at all times; however, all three must be present for a fulfilling long-term relationship.

There are numerous ways to enhance and express each component for a more satisfying relationship. It is possible to remain "in love" with your partner aside from pure infatuation. This requires some education and work on the part of the couple, but most importantly, it involves an appreciation for each other and a desire to remain together.

Lasting love is not an emotion, but a decision of two people who prioritize their relationship above the duties of daily life.
-Sarah Siders, Life consultant

I'VE LOST TRUST IN MY PARTNER.

Losing trust or confidence in your partner is devastating to the relationship. Whether it is a loss of trust in their word, their abilities, their love, or their intentions, it is a crippling blow to the integrity of a couple's connection. It undermines the very foundation of the relationship they have built together.

> **The moment there is suspicion about a person's motives, everything else becomes tainted.**
>
> -Mahatma Gandhi

When you no longer trust that your partner is telling the truth, communication suffers. Communication is the cornerstone of all good relationships. Not being able to take your partner at their word is confusing at best and frightening at worst. It undermines your reality when you have to question if someone is being sincere. Self-disclosure on your part is hindered and honestly is impaired. Making yourself vulnerable to someone who refuses to do the same and lies to you repeatedly is risky.

At this point, partners block communication, choosing to error on the side of safety. They stop sharing to protect themselves.

Furthermore, transparency is essential in any relationship. If you or your partner withholds important information from each other, it breaks down your trust. Partners sense when the other is not forthcoming.

I worked with a few clients whose partners had gambling problems. Though their partners had promised not to place money wagers of any kind, my clients found bookie's numbers in their phones, gambling tickets in their belongings, and suspicious withdrawals on their bank statements. This breach of trust bled over into other aspects of their lives. Some went so far as to question whether their partner was having an affair or even if their spouse really loved them. Everything comes into question.

Total disclosure regarding financial issues is lacking in many relationships. With money problems being a major cause of divorce, it is logical that couples need to develop and agree on a financial plan together. Spending habits, debt, priorities, and your unique relationship with money should be exposed.

Deceit inhibits trust. Individuals who lie to avoid the consequences of their actions put their relationship at risk. They know what they are doing is wrong and their partner won't approve; however, they do it anyway. When they make a choice not to communicate honestly or effectively regarding money or any other aspect of their life, they are sacrificing intimacy for isolation.

I recall an incident where a husband got a ten-thousand-dollar tax bill because his wife had cashed out her sizable 401K without his knowledge. They were having problems in their marriage prior to the event; however, her secrecy and deception reinforced his decision to get a divorce. He had lost trust in her and thus their relationship. He didn't feel she had his best interest in mind and worried about her hidden agendas. The fact that she wasn't open and authentic eventually drove him away.

Partners who don't trust each other turn into snoops. Hacking into each other's emails, reading texts, monitoring phone calls, and being suspicious of your partner erodes the relationship.

A friend once asked me to call a number she found in her husband's phone, as she suspected him of cheating on her. The woman who answered my call assured me that was not the case. She added that if my friend couldn't trust unfamiliar numbers in her partner's phone, then their relationship was doomed.

The question shouldn't be if someone is a cheater; rather it should be why do we suspect them of cheating? Why do we feel we can't trust them?

Healthy relationships consist of a certain amount of personal privacy that is essential to our well-being. Not revealing the full price you spent on a dress or that you skipped out of work early to go hit golf balls are insignificant half-truths told with the intent not to incite an argument.

It's one thing to avoid a disagreement and another to mislead your partner about important issues. Your partner should be able to trust that what you say is the truth. When we take people at their word, we have confidence in them for who they really are.

Some couples lose trust in their partner's abilities. One woman complained that her husband could no longer navigate their lives adequately. Instead of devising a plan and executing it, he seemed adrift with no particular destination. He had lost interest in his career and many of the things that used to occupy his time. He appeared to have an underlying depression that he self-medicated with alcohol. His wife lost trust in her husband's ability to self-correct and improve his condition. She was negatively impacted by his drinking and no longer felt he was the capable man she had married. When she confronted him about her fears, he shut down, insisting nothing was wrong. This intensified her lack of trust in him even further. They both knew many things were wrong with the relationship at that point.

Avoiding the truth or denying events confuses your partner. Fear and doubt set in when couples don't have accurate information to correct the problem. Peaks and valleys exist in our lives and managing them requires patience. However, when the downhill slide is apparent and shows no improvement, losing trust in our partner's abilities affects the overall relationship. It causes us to lose confidence in both the driver and direction.

I often use the analogy that it requires caution and technique when rescuing a drowning person. One has to be careful, as their panic rises, they don't take you down with them.

Regarding depression or addiction, it requires an awareness and readiness on your partner's part to reform. You can lead them down the right path, but they must go willingly. Standing by your partner and supporting them in their time of need is noble; enabling them is not. They should exhibit an effort and a desire to stop the downward spiral before it's too late. One DUI is too many; however, several are deadly. It indicates a lack of control and good judgment on the part of your partner, leaving you both exposed and in jeopardy. When you no longer trust your partner to behave responsibly and act capably, it undermines and destroys the relationship.

Perhaps the weightiest trust is that your partner truly loves you. Too many couples fake it to make it. Some say the love word to manipulate. When couples go through difficult periods, their love for each other is challenged. They struggle to have confidence in the notion that their partner really loves them.

It is a basic need and human desire to be loved and valued for who we are. Forsaking all others, people marry because they love and want to be loved. As time progresses, couples often take their love for granted.

It is important to express love to your partner throughout the relationship. Ways to demonstrate this are the following:

Physical – The power of touch is well documented. Lack of it is the biggest complaint among those who don't feel loved by their partner. Embracing in the morning, holding hands during the day, kissing on the lips as well as other favorite body parts, stroking of hair or the back and thighs, nibbling gently to tickle and incite, cuddling at night. Touching conveys to your partner that they are loved and that you want to be connected to them. Sex, intimacy, and physical displays of affection are imperative for a couple to feel attached.

Public – Public displays of affection are ways to communicate to your partner and the world that you are involved in a rewarding relationship. Though not everyone is comfortable caressing in public, there are subtler ways to connect. Some couples playfully flirt and joust with each other, while for others it is all about hand holding or eye contact. Partners that toy with each other openly send a message to outsiders that they are close. It also validates to your partner that they are important and significant. Not just at home, but wherever you go. It presents a united front full of positive respect and honor. I have heard college students mention they know couples are serious when they become "Facebook worthy." Posting you are a couple is a public declaration that you are involved and you want the world to know.

Monetary – Spending money on your partner signifies that you choose to be generous and unselfish when it comes to providing them the things that they desire. Whether it's a birthday gift or for no reason at all, being thoughtful by purchasing your partner something special goes a long way toward letting them know you love them. Doling out your hard earned money to spend on a vacation, clothing, car, jewelry, etc., for your partner illustrates you are willing to put their needs above your own.

Friendship – Treating your partner with the same kind of patience and understanding as you bestow on your dearest buddies expresses value for them as a person. Couples who respect each other's opinion and confide in one another develop an enduring friendship. As a team, couples often discover they enjoy similar activities together. Though it is healthy for couples to spend time apart on individual projects, too much time away from each other has a negative impact on the relationship. It often causes one partner to feel marginalized and alone. A mutually beneficial friendship provides your partner with the trust that you not only love them, but you love being around them as well.

Commitment – A sure way to get your partner to trust you love them is to commit yourself to them. Let them know they are exclusive. Demonstrate you have chosen to be with them and are not seeking others. Display your intentions to be with them long-term in the form of a ring, planning a wedding, relocating to be near them, living together in the same residence, or starting a family. Commit yourself to them, to their dreams, and their life. Though it's normal for couples occasionally to experience doubts regarding their relationship, commitment is about loving when it isn't easy, creating a sanctuary in the middle of chaos, and proving to your partner you will not give up when facing life's challenges.

It is impossible to talk about trust in your relationship without mentioning infidelity. When I was in graduate school, my program chair often said an affair is the symptom of a bigger problem. He encouraged us to pursue the real issues with couples and not focus on the fact one partner had strayed from the relationship.

No couple should break up simply because one partner cheated. No doubt that when your partner took another lover, they acted selfishly. They broke your wedding vows and betrayed you when they stepped outside of your relationship. They further compromised your trust when they attempted to cover it up.

You have every right to be angry, hurt, and riddled with doubt. You have been wronged in a most personal and profound way. Your partner has chosen to give the best of themselves to another, forsaking you. Rather than engage you and work on your relationship, they became preoccupied with another person. They emotionally and physically abandoned you. As bad as it seems, it isn't the end of the world. Rather, it is the beginning of enlightenment and what could be.

It is natural to blame your partner and in many cases his or her paramour. It is also wrong. No one person, no matter how seductive and alluring, can break up a fulfilling relationship. Chances are that your "cheating" partner sought attention that was absent in your relationship, inviting others inside.

Whatever the cause, you are fifty percent of the problem. It may feel better to play the victim and fault everyone except yourself. It may result in gaining sympathy from friends and family. However, if you continue to wallow in self-pity and overlook your contribution to the problem, you are doing yourself a huge injustice. Posturing and refusing to see things for what they really are will only keep you stuck.

Infidelity happens for several reasons. Like marriages, no two affairs are the same. One person may become an infidel for very different reasons than another. Affairs often provide a distraction from an unfulfilling, routine existence. One may create a fantasy world where daily stressors such as money, children, and work fade into the background. Infidelity is often used as an escape from a reality that is less than ideal. It masks the issues that exist in the primary relationship between couples. It may also be a cry for attention or help.

At the very least it is an indicator something is wrong in the relationship that needs to be addressed.

Though experts agree monogamy is unnatural for humans, they also reject the idea that once a cheater, always a cheater. Many people admit being faithful can be a struggle as we crave the security of a long term relationship and the exhilaration of a new one. To be faithful to the same mate over decades requires a conscious effort.

When partners believe their relationship is impermeable to an affair, they are clueless and naïve. Falling asleep at the wheel may result in their crashing head on into oncoming traffic

Couples who remain alert understand that long-term relationships require attention, maintenance, and work. Assuming that giving your partner the basics is enough for the long haul is immature. Threats to your marriage may arise from complacency, discontent, or mere opportunity.

The bottom line is that both bad and good marriages are susceptible to affairs, given the right circumstances.

Fidelity should not be confused with monogamy. Fidelity is loyalty, devotion and commitment. You can still feel those things for your partner and be unfaithful emotionally or physically.

What is required once adultery has occurred is the desire to remain committed to your partner and to work through the issues. It is essential to put egos aside and discover what instigated the affair in the first place. Was it a need for attention, appreciation or affirmation? Or was it the desire for distraction, excitement, or escape?

It could be as simple as a tune up – remembering who you both were and getting back to what made you such a great couple. Then again, it may be more complicated, such as a complete system check that requires uncovering childhood issues.

An affair is not a reason to split up, instead it is an opportunity for growth. To develop individually as a person as well as a couple. Infidelity doesn't have to be the end. It can provide a chance for a new beginning.

The truth is that if one partner can't get over the betrayal and moves on, they take the problems that created the affair with them. In refusing to see their participation in the predicament, they run the risk of having to repeat it all over again with someone else. They blame their ex, the opposite sex, bad luck, bad choices, or unfortunate circumstances without ever examining the role they played in the scenario.

You or your partner may have participated in some off-roading and strayed from the path. In order to move forward in a positive direction, you must:

Examine what caused you or your partner to disconnect and seek pleasure elsewhere. It is natural for people to go toward the light and avoid the dark. Shine a light on the dark and deal with it head on.

Determine your role in the predicament. You both created the mess you find yourself in either directly or indirectly. Uncover the part you played in the affair and own it.

Get rid of your ego. Because someone had the bad judgment to stray doesn't mean they chose someone better than you. They chose different. Discover why. Empathy and understanding should prevail.

Let go of the bitterness. Recognizing your contribution to the problem will help to eliminate some of the resentment toward your partner. This is imperative if you have children together.

Embrace the idea that because your partner acted in an unloving manner does not mean they don't still love you. They are wrestling with their own issues from childhood and beyond. Help them get the assistance they need and you do the same.

Transcend the experience. Once you grasp the underlying issues, you may or may not want to proceed together. What both of you decide to do should be an educated choice. Respect what happened and why it happened without judgment. It doesn't do either of you any good to demean the other. When you do that, your character and integrity are as compromised as the person you are disparaging.

The bottom line is that affairs happen. They don't have to result in divorce. It is a choice that requires introspection, understanding, and forgiveness. Some couples emerge from the experience stronger than ever, while for others there is no turning back. Whatever is decided should take considerable deliberation and reflection with egos and self-pity aside.

WE HAVE LOST RESPECT FOR EACH OTHER.

Respect is a verb. You know when someone respects you by the way they treat you and speak about you to others. In most relationships, respect is implied. However, the lack of it becomes obvious and at a significant cost. Ways we disrespect our partner may leave them feeling unloved, unappreciated, and misunderstood. Partners may project those feelings on each other due to their own frustrations and misgivings. Either way, when these perceptions are not addressed, resentment sets in.

Treating your partner with respect

When one partner ignores the other, they are acting disrespectfully. Whether they disregard their partner's feelings, needs, accomplishments, or their company in a room full of people, ignoring is dismissing. When someone is overlooked, they feel unimportant and insignificant. Their voice is not heard, their deeds are not appreciated, and they are left feeling unloved and unwanted. This may set off a chain of events that irreparably damage the relationship.

When individuals feel unacknowledged, they tend to act out in self-destructive ways. They may engage in addictive behaviors, such as gambling and drinking, or seek attention elsewhere by having affairs. The partner being ignored feels justified in their negative behavior because they perceive themselves as being undervalued. I've heard men express that even though they provide for their family, their wives spend most of their time and attention on the children. Feeling disrespected and unappreciated, they seek pleasure and gratitude elsewhere.

Conversely, I have heard women complain that their husbands avoid them while traveling for work, golfing, or attending sporting events. While these women maintain the household, their men engage in separate activities that consume their time and attention. In both cases, these individuals are feeling ignored and unappreciated.

In childhood development, toddlers experience a stage called parallel play, where children will individually play with their toys while sitting side by side. As they mature, interactive play develops. When partners disregard each other while going about their daily routine, they are engaging in parallel play. Neither experiences a rewarding relationship. They coexist in a partnership that frustrates them both. Rather than ask for the attention and love that they need, they act out in ways that confuse and disappoint each other.

Eventually the disregard develops into disrespect for the relationship. When the negative behaviors continue, self-respect suffers. Engaging in self-destructive or addictive behaviors takes its toll and guilt sets in. Negative feelings and doubts emerge, allowing the relationship to disintegrate.

Speaking about your partner with respect

Speaking ill of your partner is public is the ultimate form of disrespect. First, they are not given the courtesy of knowing how poorly you portray them to others. Second, they aren't there to defend themselves. Often times the unsuspecting party has no clue as to the disparaging remarks made about them by their partner. These negative comments, now etched in other's minds, have a way of manifesting themselves into the couple's lives. Thoughts become words and words become actions.

I counseled a woman and asked her to recall the defining moment when she knew her marriage was over. Her most hurtful memory was not the most obvious. While debating to leave her husband, her best friend said, "He doesn't adore you." What she already felt in her gut but had never admitted became undeniable. Forced to acknowledge her fears, she decided to end her marriage. Her partner didn't love and respect her the way she needed. Their husbands were in the same poker group. My client suspected her husband had berated her to his card-playing buddies. Though they had many questionable incidents leading up to their divorce, this was non-negotiable.

What some may call insignificant was the final straw for her. Instead of working on the marriage and keeping their issues private, her husband had verbally disrespected her to his friends. Rather than confront her with his feelings, he confused her about his intentions and then spoke ill of her behind her back. He would engage her just enough to remain in the relationship and then tell others he didn't want to be with her. He set her up to be humiliated, as she was the last to know. She no longer trusted his intentions regarding her.

I worked with another client who, while debating to leave her husband, sent a text to her girlfriend that read, "The only reason I am in this marriage is for the money."

That was the defining moment for her husband to seek a divorce. Aware of their ongoing marital issues, he stayed and fought to keep the family intact. Once he read those words, whether she really meant them or not, he was finished. He wanted to represent more in a relationship than merely a paycheck. My client couldn't be as honest with him as she was her friend, and once he read that unfiltered message, he moved on.

Couples do this to one another and it makes everyone look bad. As we mature, we realize there is her story, his story, and the truth lies somewhere in between. When we repeatedly complain about our partners and remain with them, it reflects badly on us. Individuals either lose respect for our word or our ability to modify the situation. It is very telling about your character to speak poorly about someone you love.

Women often seek sympathy and attention when they say terrible things about their husbands. They sometimes portray themselves as saints, sacrificing for the children and being the glue that holds the family together. They tend to avoid responsibility for the problems in their relationship, failing to acknowledge their own faults. Finding it difficult to recognize their insecurities and shortcomings, they blame him.

Rather than engage in self-awareness to discover how they may be contributing to his bad behavior, they prefer to play the victim. While in this role and eliciting responses from individuals who validate them, these women feed their egos and sense of entitlement.

Men tend to make excuses as to why their relationship is unsuccessful, while seeking attention elsewhere. They will complain about their dissatisfying relationship, claiming it lacks love and intimacy. Often calling their wife a roommate or dependent, they diminish the marriage by speaking in demeaning and unloving ways about their partner.

It appears in these instances they want the security of their marriage, yet seek the excitement of a new relationship. Portraying themselves as trapped and unhappy, they find sympathetic females who will give them what they want. Thus they have their cake and eat it, too. They justify their need to have an affair by making their partner less than.

We are all familiar with the couple that spars and fights as foreplay. They are loyal and united as partners, defending each other publicly. They would never speak ill about their partner to outsiders because they are a team. Team players are not always in agreement and they sometimes feel animosity toward each other; however, they protect their relationship in a unified fashion. They respectfully defend their marriage while contradicting each other. Regardless of their bickering, we are acutely aware of the love and respect they share.

I would rather someone leave me than repeatedly speak ill of me to others. When partners disrespect each other by disparaging their love in public, it is devastating to the relationship. I wouldn't continue a friendship with someone who spoke negatively about me behind my back; I won't accept that from a partner either.

That doesn't mean I worry about being popular or liked. It means, if I am in a devoted relationship, then I want my partner to behave lovingly and respectfully toward me. It is acceptable to joke about character flaws or take jabs at personality traits; however, it shouldn't be done in a malicious way. The context in which it is presented is important.

- Respect that your partner is not you. They are different from you and that is okay.

- Respect your partner for who they are and what they bring to the relationship.

- Respect your partner enough not to berate them to others. It's one thing to be angry with them and vent about it to a friend, it's another to repeatedly attack their character. Don't make them look bad in public.

- Respect your partner enough to go to them first with any issues you are having with them. Don't go behind their back.

- Respect your partner enough to interact with them beyond the basic communication of who is going to pick up the kids and what's for dinner.

- Respect your partner enough to adore them in public as well as in private.

- Respect your partner enough to end the relationship before you make a fool of them and yourself. Public humiliation is unnecessary.

- Respect your partner enough to love them beyond the relationship even after it has ended. This is the beginning of the good divorce.

WE JUST DONT HAVE ANYTHING IN COMMON ANYMORE.

This is a predicament that happens to couples with the best intentions. In most cases, it progresses slowly and by the time it is fully realized, it is often too late.

This dilemma recurs throughout the life span. It is common with couples in their twenties during the courtship phase, with couples in their forties after starting a family, as well as with empty nesters in their fifties.

Developmentally speaking, a twenty-something's task is to cultivate a career and seek out a suitable companion. While accomplishing these goals, individuals may fall in love and then decide the universe is sending them in different directions. Those same individuals in their thirties eventually select a mate, settle down, and have a family.

The thirties are about becoming proficient in a career, establishing a home, and having children. How effectively couples integrate children into their marriage is a predictor as to marital success in their forties.

Children change the dynamic of a relationship. There are those who contend children strengthen a marriage and those who claim they weaken it. Negatively or positively, for better or worse, children have a tremendous impact on marriages.

As a couple, you experience a completely different reality. It is a balancing act that requires constant adjusting. Some navigate through it with ease while others fail.

I have heard men state the problem with relationships is that women want to change men and men want women to stay the same. When couples first meet, women fall in love, often thinking they can improve their man over time. Men fall in love with women, thinking they won't change after having children. Neither is an option.

Men want their partner to remain as sexy and interesting as she was in the courtship stage. However, women who give up their careers to be stay-at-home moms face difficult challenges. The dynamic professional woman transforms into a preoccupied mommy.

Many women who devote themselves to their families complain of fatigue and tedium. They often choose to dress more for comfort and less for success. They put their children's needs before their own and make them a priority over their husband. At the end of the day, some end up frazzled and resentful that the responsibility of managing the household rests on them.

Though this scenario is not typical of every relationship, it happens far too often. Many women who were taught to be independent, trained professionals have difficulty transitioning into the role of full-time mother. Children become their sole focus, to the exclusion of their men. They become annoyed when their men go off to work to interact with the real world while they are left to care for everyone and everything. The woman who once wore skinny jeans and heels now wears modern-day sweats with a bad attitude.

When men then focus their interests elsewhere with sports, recreational toys, or beers with the guys, conflict arises. If not corrected, it is the beginning of the end. A friend of mine once asked me why couples seem to get a little crazy in their forties and split up. I said it's because many recognize that the choices they made haven't brought them happiness. The person they married, the career they selected, the house they purchased, and the children they had didn't bring them the pleasure they had hoped. At that point, things seem to unravel. Aware they are entering middle age, they either make some adjustments for a happier life or leave the relationship in an attempt to realize their dreams.

Whether children enhance or destroy the connection between partners is up to the couple. Some tips for success are:

Couples should have a good babysitter they can depend on when they need to get away and have fun.

They must remember to date and love on each other. If they don't, someone else will. Partners need to be as mindful and deliberate with each other as when they first fell in love. All couples desire a romantic connection and when it is absent, their relationship suffers. Be careful not to let everyday life interfere with your loving intentions.

Your relationship came before the children.

It should remain your priority while you and your partner set boundaries for developing a family. Discussing these guidelines before the baby arrives is important. Never think that because you had children with your partner they will remain with you regardless of how badly you treat them. Individuals crave love and respect and many won't compromise those things for the sake of the children.

It is imperative for couples to agree on the rules and the consequences for raising the children.

Too many couples battle over when to discipline and how to execute the punishment. When one parent undermines the other regarding modifying their children's behavior, it causes conflict. A client of mine said his ability to raise his children increased after the divorce because his parental input was no longer dismissed or sabotaged by his wife.

Assuming couples have navigated their relationship through their twenties, thirties, and forties, the next significant hurdle for partners is becoming empty nesters. Some see this challenge approaching and develop interests together to replace the attention and focus previously dedicated to the children. Others see it as their window of escape.

Empty nest couples are faced with reinventing their relationship post-children or going their separate ways. Either direction typically comes as more of surprise to their friends than it does to their partner.

A spike in the divorce rate of those over 60 is now being reported. These late life divorces reflect a change in our society. Whereas in previous generations, couples would co-exist, living parallel but separate lives, they seem more reluctant to do so today. Considering they may have another thirty years to live, they want the years remaining to be as fulfilling as possible. They want to be able to enjoy their twilight years before they are too old to enjoy them.

Post careers and childrearing responsibilities, these dissatisfied couples have become strangers. No longer in the traditional roles that once defined them and their relationships, they don't relate to one another. Their common goals of raising a family and establishing careers have been met.

Quite simply, they must readjust to this new phase in life by developing a new connection with each other. They need to establish new goals, as individuals as well as partners. Couples should acquire innovative activities and new interests to be utilized in their free time. Otherwise, boredom sets in and these individuals become stagnant or restless.

As we develop, our relationship criteria evolves. Unlike young love, where there are few expectations other than to be loved in return, mature love comes with conditions. Individuals may seek out others who possess the same educational level they do, or surround themselves with people from the same socioeconomic group. When divorced or widowed, some choose to date partners with children to raise while others prefer a partner who is free to travel.

Whether it is an old relationship that needs updating, or a new one we seek, individuals cultivate standards they feel must be present for a successful partnership. It might be based on more meaningful communication, increased energy, additional laughter, or intensified affection. In some cases, it's more money.

Whatever advanced measures we require, it's no longer as simple as loving someone. It's quite common for couples who are divorcing to say they still love their ex; however, they both feel they are better off without the other. Loving someone doesn't guarantee a harmonious existence with them.

SECTION THREE

Where Do You Want To Go?

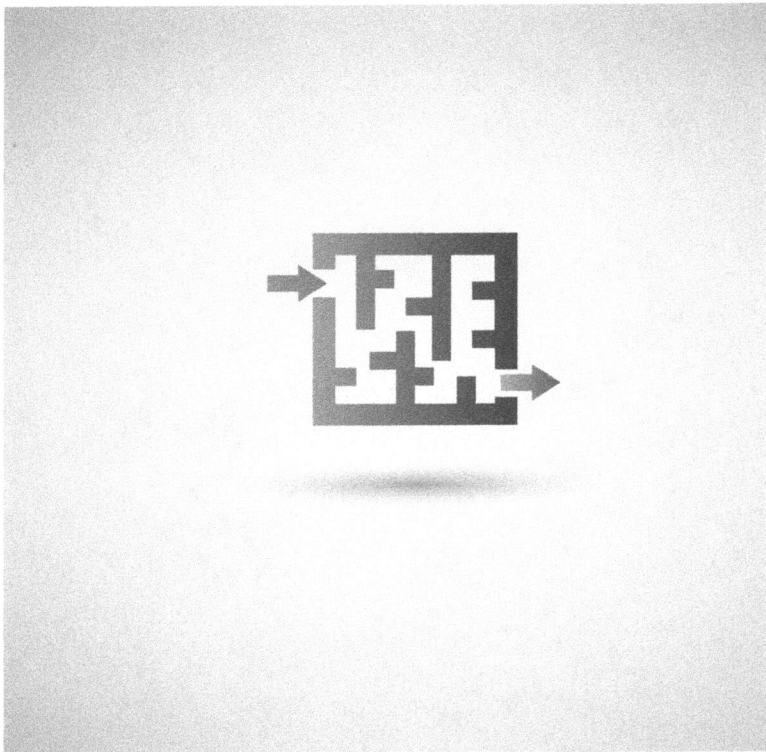

SECTION THREE

Where Do You Want To Go?

The first half of this book is concerned with acknowledging that you are at a fork in the road regarding your relationship. As well as trying to decipher why and how you got there, it also promotes assessing where you have been and examines your marital issues in detail.

A Fork in the Road encourages anyone who is contemplating leaving a long-term relationship to pause and not run merely for the sake of running. Instead it suggests reflecting on the relationship in its entirety and not just the last piece of it. By putting it in perspective and comprehending that you are fifty percent of the equation, you avoid assigning blame. Rather, try to understand your relationship problems and their origin.

Should you decide to proceed with a divorce, understand your motives for terminating the relationship, evaluate the consequences, and devise a plan for going forward.

It is important to ask questions, seek solutions, and ascertain you have done everything possible before ending your relationship. The emotion surfing, soul searching, gut wrenching journey is a solo one. However, that doesn't mean you must go it alone. At times a third party may offer additional insight, whether it is a therapist or a friend. Once you have suffered all of the indecision and agony concerning your happily ever after... consider the following.

Generate a side-by-side list of the things you will lose in a divorce, as well as the things you will gain.

LOSE   GAIN

_____   _____

_____   _____

_____   _____

_____   _____

_____   _____

_____   _____

_____   _____

_____   _____

Consider taking four additional steps for clarity:

BRING IN A THIRD PARTY

You see it one way, your partner sees it another, and then there is the reality of the situation regardless who is right or wrong. A neutral party has the objectivity to see things without emotional attachment or hurt. Often times a therapist or counselor facilitates individuals to consider a position without their becoming defensive.

Counselors speak the truth without blame or an agenda. They observe what is happening and report on it. This transparency is required to dig deep and cut through the layers of trouble. Counselors are professionals who:

- Gather information from both parties

- Clarify problems and issues

- Offer insight into a situation to enlighten both parties

- Provide directives intended to educate both parties

- Motivate people to change

- Assist in the aftermath

Think of a therapist as a mechanic. They have the tools to diagnose the problems in the relationship. They help fix them, providing there is a desire and effort on the part of the couple.

ENGAGE IN A TRIAL SEPARATION

I recommend this for all couples before divorce. Some complain it is too costly and inconvenient. That may be true; however, if one person initiates the divorce and then has remorse, the price for that blunder is immeasurable. It may result in a lifetime of regret.

A trial separation has several benefits:

It allows both individuals a time out. A quiet place to calm down, cool off, and think. Each person goes off into their separate corners where time and space allow them the opportunity to contemplate without interruption. It provides neutral ground where emotions aren't so highly charged and the immediacy of a response is diminished. Individuals are discouraged from shooting from the hip and discharging ugly accusations. It gives each person time to breathe and time to reflect.

It has the benefit of taking both parties back in time. Should they choose, they may court, date, and communicate with each other at a safe distance. They have the opportunity to start over, to rekindle the flame that was dowsed in marital discord. They have the occasion to flirt with each other and make deliberate attempts to be together. They aren't forced to tolerate each other in a situation that is no longer sufferable.

It allows time for the counseling to work. The therapeutic sessions and ideas may be integrated without the pressure of crowding each other at home. Introspection is easier without having your partner constantly under foot. Reading materials can be digested at leisure without posing a threat to your partner.

A trial separation is a glimpse at what a divorce looks like. It separates couples, allowing them to feel the loss of being apart. For people with children, it gives them an idea of what it is going to be like not waking up with them every morning. Home is not the same. The person who moves out gets a real taste of what it is like to lose the belongings they have acquired over the years. The separation has a negative financial impact on the couple, giving them a preview of what divorce will cost them monetarily. It clarifies for many if they want to divorce or work things out.

SEEK INDIVIDUAL COUNSELING

With the disintegration of a relationship, we break a bit as well. Raw with emotion, we say and do things out of character. When individuals contemplate splitting up their family, they wrestle with a wide range of sentiments. Internally they are battling demons while externally they are forced to deal with daily pressures. Add to that the opinions and judgments of outsiders, it's a wonder anyone survives a divorce.

Individual counseling is important for a couple of reasons. First, it forces the individual to look within and grasp their sense of self. A divorce is never one person's responsibility. Recognizing your involvement and how you may better yourself is a bonus for everyone, most of all you.

I worked with a male client who got a divorce and then realized he functioned no better for it. His underlying problem was depression. Though not the singular cause of his divorce, it was a major contributing factor. Once single again, he found he wasn't any happier alone. Believing the divorce would bring him peace, he failed to experience any relief. What was supposed to lighten his load only made him sadder. He had blamed the marriage for his unhappiness while never confronting his clinical depression. He eventually had to deal with his situation before he could move on to another relationship.

Similarly, I've counseled female clients who blamed their divorce on their husband's cheating. When I mention that an affair is a symptom of a bigger problem, they prefer to point fingers at him. Blaming is easy because everyone knows infidelity is wrong. However, upon further investigation, these women admit to eating dinner with their children before their husband got home from work. They also confess to going to bed when their children did, leaving their partner to fend for himself. Hiding behind being a busy mother, they report being too exhausted for sex. These women completely ignored their husbands and then faulted them for seeking affection elsewhere.

Another benefit of individual counseling is to determine if there are lingering childhood issues that prevent you from enjoying a healthy adult relationship. Healing childhood wounds are necessary to understand and modify your reaction to certain situations. Individuals bring their past experiences and expectations into the marriage and are often clueless as to their nature. As children we observe how our parents deal with conflict and often times we emulate that as adults. Shutting down, stonewalling, verbal abuse, physical violence, manipulation, and jealousy are a few of the things we may have learned. Childhood issues such as fear of abandonment, attitudes toward sex, coping skills, and managing stress are other areas to explore when relationships fail. Patterns regarding relationships develop and should be explored. It begins and ends with you.

MAKE A LIST OF "MUSTS"

Make a list of at least three "musts" in order for you to stay with your partner. Under each "must," list four or five reasons why it is necessary and important. Examples:

My partner must have dinner with the family at least four times a week.
- It demonstrates he is interested in me and the children and is making us a priority.
- It will help us bond as a family.
- I won't resent him for leaving me alone during meal preparation and clean up.
- It will eliminate his having drinks at the sports club with his buddies.

My partner and I must have date night one night per week.
- This will allow for adult conversation without interruption.
- It will set the stage for intimacy.
- It will encourage dating and loving behavior.
- It will remind us of a time when we choose to be together alone.
- It will allow us the opportunity to dress up and impress the other.

My partner must stop gambling on football games.
- It will help our financial situation.
- It will prevent having to hide bank statements that reveal withdrawals for gambling purposes.
- It will prevent having to deal with angry mood swings when losing.
- It will create more transparency in the relationship.
- It will create more trust in the marriage.

Are these things attainable or even realistic?

Is your partner a willing participant who will
accommodate your "musts"?

When all else fails... DIVORCE COUNSELING IS RECOMMENDED

Knowing how to be divorced is almost impossible because divorce is complicated on many levels. What works for one couple doesn't work for another. As I mentioned previously, where you stand depends on where you look. Though your perception has become your reality, it isn't necessarily the truth. A counselor can help you sort through things to construct a more authentic picture.

After individuals have obsessed about their situation, worked through several problems, and have taken appropriate measures to improve, a divorce still remains difficult.

Most everyone seeking a divorce meets with an attorney to seek legal advice in order to protect themselves. They become educated about the divorce laws in the state where they reside. These professionals advocate for their rights. They want the property and assets divided fairly and they want access to their children. A legal divorce is fairly straightforward today.

Unfortunately, the unhealthy emotions prior to, during, and after the divorce may persist for a lifetime. Often times the blame, resentment, anger, bitterness, and competition persevere well beyond an acceptable limit. I am aware of children who haven't had contact with a parent for years because they sided with the other. More than one of my clients has agonized about having to see their ex and his new partner at an event for their children. The ex remains in the tension zone, engaged in name calling at best and threats of violence at worst.

It benefits no one to continue fighting a battle that no longer exists. The divorce signifies the end. It is the final nail in the coffin. Most divorced couples never resurrect their intimate relationship and need assistance with how to move on in a positive manner.

A counselor helps individuals heal. Sometimes it takes an outsider to highlight the good that came from the relationship. Healthy children, a house that was paid off, interesting adventures, mutual friends, and even good recipes. There is a silver lining in most every partnership, even the most toxic. Perhaps the only benefit was a lesson learned.

One may profit spiritually from negative experiences, like touching a hot stove when you are a child. Once burned, you will not intentionally do it again because of the pain it caused.

A counselor will help you reframe the most difficult experiences into a valuable message. It is a stepping stone to a better place. A launching pad for growth and development. Learning to be grateful for having had the experience helps you realize the ways you advanced beyond it.

SECTION FOUR

How Do You Get a Good Divorce?

SECTION FOUR

How Do You Get a Good Divorce?

You have done all you can to address and correct problems in the relationship and are still unhappy. Sometimes the best thing you can do is to leave it.

Remaining in a marriage overcome with obstacles and life-sucking interactions is no longer an option. For the sake of your welfare and everyone involved, divorce is a reasonable outcome. Certain relationships are lethal and there are times when it is beneficial to your mental or physical wellbeing to get out. When circumstances become intolerable (not just unpleasant), splitting up may be the best alternative. No one, not even a therapist or counselor, can tell you if divorce is the right answer for you. You must determine what is true for your situation. Seek answers, take your time, and avoid being reactionary.

Intelligibility is key while sorting through a long list of unwanted emotions. Taking an alternative route in life may sound intriguing; however, it may lead you off a cliff. Map out your course with precision.

You will never regret having done all you can to understand and save your marriage. You will be eternally sorry if you gave up too soon.

Once you confirm that a divorce is your best choice, own it and arrange for what follows. Under the best of circumstances, divorce is difficult. It is life event filled with loss.

The material loss is evident. Assets are split 50/50. Financial security and lifestyle are impacted. There is also the physical loss of your partner. Regarding children, the forfeiture of being able to spend unscheduled time with them, along with all holidays and birthdays, is a significant cost.

The loss of in-laws and some friends is substantial as well. There is emotional damage concerning self-confidence and the fear of never finding love again as well as the loss of your identity as a couple. Life as you knew it is over. Your concept of "home" will change whether you are the one who stays in the house or not.

Recognizing the losses and consequences that surround divorce does not lessen them. Just as it took effort and sacrifice to build a relationship, it takes that same persistence and determination to end it. You will suffer the penalties of divorce and crawl over broken glass to get to the other side. Your goal should be to cross over with the least amount of pain possible. Divorce should be the only good solution to your relationship impasse.

Now it is up to you whether to get a good divorce or a bad one. It is a conscious choice.

No doubt you will grieve. The seven stages of grief have been described as the following:

- Shock
- Denial
- Pain
- Guilt
- Anger
- Depression
- Acceptance

You will experience all of these, slipping in and out of them at various times and in no particular order. There will be days when one or two of them will bring you to your knees. It is your job to work through them. Succumbing to being a victim is not in your best interest. Other than acceptance, these stages of grief will drag you under if manifested for too long.

SHOCK

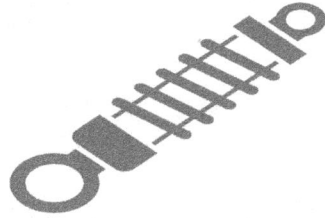

No matter how often you and your partner have threatened divorce, it is shocking when it finally happens. Though you have accepted the inevitability of it, announcing it to family, friends, and co-workers makes it real.

The blow that divorce delivers is lessened when you understand why it was the best solution and believe it was inevitable. Having determined the cause without blame diminishes the disappointment. Knowing you have done all you could do to rescue a relationship that was unsalvageable helps reduce the denial regarding your divorce.

Several of my friends, who should never have gotten married in the first place, ended up divorced. They battled constantly, upsetting their children, who would retreat to their rooms. At parties the wife would unleash her pent up anger after a few glasses of wine and a fight would ensue. One where she wept in the bathroom as her girlfriends consoled her. Friends of the couple were relieved to hear they were finally getting a divorce, joking that one would be killed while the other went to prison. It was a coin toss as to which partner was which. Family and friends prefer to see a combative couple go through a divorce rather than be on an episode of *Snapped*.

The shock of divorce has been described as a feeling of preparing to jump off a diving board and not wanting to swim. A paralysis of "what now?" sets in. Fear of taking the next step and not knowing where to go or what to do emerges.

Shock and denial are often temporary states of mind that numb the individual to their current situation. When emotions are in turmoil and anxiety about the future is at its peak, shock can prevent us from spinning out of control. Couples fear loneliness, their loss of identity, change in lifestyle, and what the future holds.

With your equilibrium challenged, it will take time and effort to regain a sense of stability. In the meantime, shock is warranted. Going through the motions without feeling them so intensely is a way of coping with the unfamiliar.

The newness and gravity of the situation may be overwhelming. Going from being a couple to being single again takes some getting used to. The decision to stop wearing your wedding ring, the division of household items, seeking out a new place to live, no longer going to social events together - this is all a jolt to the system. In the beginning, what will eventually become routine is foreign and frightening.

DENIAL

Denial and shock go side by side. As we try to wrap our head around what has happened to us, denial protects us. Similar to exploding airbags in crashes, denial softens the blow. The numbing affect shields us from injury until we regroup and collect ourselves.

Our mind and body reject the loss as we fantasize about possibly getting back together again. It is normal to experience these emotions and respect how they shelter us.

Shock and denial are initially useful, and any damage resulting from them is a result of hanging onto them for too long. Denial that your lifestyle hasn't changed and that life will continue as before puts you at risk.

Consider the single mother who was a stay-at-home mom and accustomed to living a certain lifestyle. Even with a fair settlement and child support, she will need to secure employment. One of my clients depleted a million dollars in ten years through questionable investments and her refusal to work full time. Financially insolvent, she was left with no assets, no savings, and no retirement plan. Denial regarding her change of status cost her dearly.

Financial advisors warn divorcees and widows that unless the family home is paid for, keeping it is their biggest drain and liability. Unwilling to relinquish their residence or cut back, women often find themselves in financial jeopardy. Attempting to maintain life as before without the same source of income is a form of denial. They are simply delaying the inevitable by spending their settlement on sustaining what was. This false sense of security eventually disappears and they are left having to deal with the severity of their financial situation.

Denial is not only seen in the financial aspect of the divorce. It is also seen with respect to how couples now deal with the holidays. Couples who are separated will often reconcile during the holidays because it is too painful to experience them alone.

A friend of mine was dating a man who was in the middle of a divorce. They went out on New Year's Eve only to run into his ex and her girlfriends. The ex who lived forty minutes away had intentionally sought him out and wept publically the entire evening. Though he was living in another community and dating other women, she sabotaged his evening by her denial that they were divorcing.

Straddling the fence is not good for the individuals in a relationship. Shock and denial are useful in the early stages of the split because they protect couples from experiencing the hurt and uncertainty so deeply.

Eventually those feelings must give way to a hope for a new beginning. Living in purgatory is difficult and emotionally draining. The goal is not to hang on to the past in desperation, but rather to transition to a better future. This should be accomplished as fast and smoothly as possible.

All the stages of grief are normal and are part of the healing process. When our loss is great as in divorce or death, we tend to experience the stages more severely and it takes longer to shift from one stage to the other.

PAIN

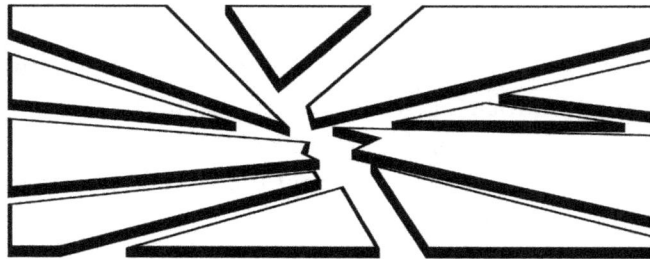

At some point in our journey, we must experience the full extent of the hurt. It's normal for individuals to avoid pain at all cost. We are biologically wired to seek shade when it's hot, cover up when we are cold, and eat when we are hungry. Avoiding discomfort is natural. However, after experiencing a significant loss, it is important to mourn. Denying the pain or repressing it will only result in it materializing at a most inconvenient and unexpected time. We need to consciously deal with it and release it.

Funerals are vital for a reason. They allow for loved ones to heal. First, there is a fixed point in time when reality hits that the person is gone. There is no going back, no gray area, no doubt. The funeral and burial marks the finality of your earthly relationship with the departed.

Second, the service allows loved ones to mourn together. To laugh, cry, and express their thoughts and feelings about the deceased. A funeral is an acceptable place for loved ones to publically hurt, wail, hug, and unload.

Third, the ceremony and gathering is a show of love and support. The grieving person is showered with sympathy and empathy in a helping environment. It is a unifying experience as opposed to a dividing one. It allows the individuals left behind to feel appreciated and acknowledged. Funerals make room for the pain and signify the end.

To feel the pain and loss of your relationship, I recommend the following:

- Go to a favorite spot you both enjoyed and reflect on your time together
- Listen to your favorite songs you experienced as a couple
- Look at photos of when you two were together in happier times
- Watch sad movies that make you cry
- Confront the pain in order to release it
- Walk over the burning coals to get to the other side

This should not take place in the early stages of your divorce when things are still too raw. It is something to consider when you are strong enough and ready to be done with it.

Some find it cruel and unnecessary to relive these emotions. However, once they are fully practiced and released, they no longer carry the dread and power associated with them. You no longer have to avoid sentimental thoughts or moments. By challenging yourself and your reserve you will conquer your fears and put them to rest. Now you can move on with no barriers.

A friend of mine invited all of the friends who supported her during her divorce to a dinner at the country club where she and her ex-husband had belonged. It was a ceremonial way of saying good-bye to him and terminating her membership at the same time. Much like a funeral, she decided to grieve publically alongside family and friends. For her, it signified the end. She took control, defining her final moment from which to let her marriage go.

GUILT

Guilt is a self-imposed emotion. It is something we do to ourselves.

No doubt our parents, friends, and children impose guilt upon us; however, we are the ones who must receive it. Guilt is a wonderful motivator for a child when given from a loving caretaker. Used in small doses, it can be very effective. As adults with our own value system and sense of right and wrong, we are given the alternative to accept the guilt imposed on us for it to be useful.

My mother attempted to guilt me into staying with my ex-husband. She went so far as to threaten me, stating that if I left him, she would choose his side. This could have intimidated me and made me feel bad about my decision. However, I didn't believe she would follow through with her declaration, and as an adult I had already made up my mind. Appreciating that she wasn't married to my ex and incapable of understanding my decision to divorce, I called her bluff. Though she attempted to assign guilt to me, I refused to receive it.

When individuals attempt to make us do something they want, they resort to using guilt. In a divorce there is plenty of guilt to throw around. Some examples are:

- Guilt one carries by just being who you are. You aren't good enough or worthy enough or strong enough. You just aren't enough.

- Guilt for not having tried hard enough in the relationship. If I had only done this or that… would things be different?

- Guilt of breaking up a home is an enormous burden. Leaving your partner to fend for themselves is difficult. Forcing children to adjust to the daily inconveniences and long term results of a split is tough.

- Guilt of being divorced or a single parent is ever present in society.

- Guilt when moving on with your life if your partner is still stuck in the past.

- Guilt surrounding being happy if your partner is not.

- Guilt associated with having to reject someone you once loved.

- Guilt affiliated with the in-laws. What once was considered family is now considered distant at best and adversarial at worst.

Guilt is a good indicator of how well you are managing your state of affairs. It reminds us to do well by others. If we have done the right thing, our guilt will be diminished or nonexistent.

If, on the other hand, we have been self-serving or manipulative, guilt becomes a factor. Guilt is a good barometer of what is fair. In the event you didn't take advantage of your partner and they treated you equitably in return, the guilt will be marginalized. However, if the opposite is true and you and your ex are spiteful and contentious, anger will result.

ANGER

There will be anger. It is a justifiable reaction to someone who has disappointed or hurt you. You will be angry that life isn't fair. Your hopes and dreams failed to materialize and you are entitled to be pissed off.

Anger is a natural response to not getting what you want from a relationship. As a couple, you both made promises to each other in the form of vows. You vowed to be together until death. You created a family with the idea that you would both be united to enjoy it. Promises were broken and you responded by being irate.

We get angry with our partner when we feel that they are being unfair, or when they are not meeting our needs. Anger develops from the belief or frustration that we are being mistreated. When we perceive our partner as indifferent, uncaring or working against us, frustration easily erupts into anger. Often times, one partner wants the other to change, when in reality it is their own attitude that needs to be modified.

Anger follows when individuals feel stress or pain. Both of those emotions are magnified in a divorce and as a result, anger becomes the typical response when one partner doesn't get their way. Albert Ellis, founder of the Institute for Rational-Emotive Therapy, contends that anger is one of the most damaging of all human emotions. He believed:

- Anger is a result of unrealistic expectations and "shoulds."
- Anger spills over into other areas of your life.
- Depression and anxiety are due to increased tensions in your life from anger.
- Anger, depression, and anxiety may evoke negative responses from others in your life, causing self-criticism and low self-esteem.
- All of the above emotions can negatively impact your relationships with others.

Individuals are capable of managing their anger by controlling their thoughts. Anger is a choice and it is something we can regulate. Our perception of a situation with our partner is what triggers our anger. We assume or perceive they are out to harm us. That may or may not be the case.

By reducing our emotional feelings and physiological arousal through cognitive and relaxation techniques, we learn how to manage our anger more effectively.

Also, attempting to understand our emotions and being able to reframe a situation helps with anger management.

I was initially angry upon discovering that my ex-husband had cheated on me, as anyone would be. However, after the shock wore off, I decided to use it as a tool to discover what was missing in our relationship and why he had chosen to put our marriage at risk. I reframed the situation from being the worst kind of betrayal to a valuable learning experience.

I discovered that while I was focused and excited about opening a new business, he felt ignored. He was jealous that I was self-employed and that he had to work for a large and impersonal company. He had gained weight and didn't feel like the hot virile guy he was when we first married. Many would say those are excuses for bad behavior, and they would be right. That doesn't negate the fact he had felt all of those things and I had been insensitive to them.

My ex was unable to express these feelings because he was ashamed of them. He is not one to disclose or share his feelings and he believed they would subside with time. They didn't. Furthermore, once they were acknowledged, he was open to counseling.

My point is that I can choose to be angry over the fact he was unfaithful to me or I can recognize his cry for help. When I obsessed about his disrespect and disregard for me, it made me angry. Instead, I chose to focus on the cause, not the crime. Though we decided to end our marriage, we remained very good friends. Putting things in perspective and exercising forgiveness are both essential components to getting a good divorce.

It does no good to place blame and play the victim. The good divorce is about being able to see the entirety of your relationship without assigning fault. It is what it is and you both had a part in it.

You may not be able to avoid things that enrage you in the process of getting a divorce, but you can learn to control your reactions to them. Also, you will not be able to change your partner in the process. You are in control of you. For the sake of your children and your future, understanding and forgiveness are vital. Moving beyond the anger is required for a good divorce and imperative for a new beginning.

DEPRESSION

The dean of my graduate program often stated that depression is anger turned inward. This is evident in those who are chronically irritable. Grumpy partners who bark at their spouse and suck the joy from the relationship are often experiencing depression. Social withdrawal and a sense of hopelessness and helplessness are present. The depressed individual experiences a sense of worthlessness and low self-esteem.

Depression may be situational, as in response to a loss or event, or it may be chronic and require medication. In getting a good divorce, it's helpful to understand there will be prompts throughout the divorce that will make you feel sad. That's normal and they will subside with time. Common triggers are:

- Unfamiliar surroundings if you are the one who moved out
- The holidays
- Significant events you shared together, such as an annual festival or an art show
- Restaurants, clubs, or vacation spots you frequented together
- Loss of family, friends, and your previous social network
- Certain TV programs or songs can activate a longing for the past
- Recognizing what you had and what you lost
- Not waking up every morning with your children

- Loss of lifestyle
- Loneliness
- Witnessing your ex move on
- Being forced into social situations with your ex due to the children

There are many things to grieve when a relationship ends. Even after people move on, it is normal to miss certain things about your ex. After my ex and I split and had married other partners whom we both agreed were more suitable for us, we admitted missing parts of our relationship. He missed golfing with me and I missed skiing with him. The admission of missing something you appreciated about the other helps to foster a good divorce.

Certain individuals require counseling and sometimes medication to get them through the rough spots. When anxiety or depression becomes overwhelming to the point of not being able to sleep or function, a physician should be consulted to help the individual manage their life better. Being constantly tearful or hysterical in response to the divorce may require temporary intervention from an outside source. A counselor assists with coping strategies, and a physician may prescribe medication to eliminate dramatic mood swings.

The approach in dealing with depression during this time should include seeking outside help rather than blaming your ex.

ACCEPTANCE

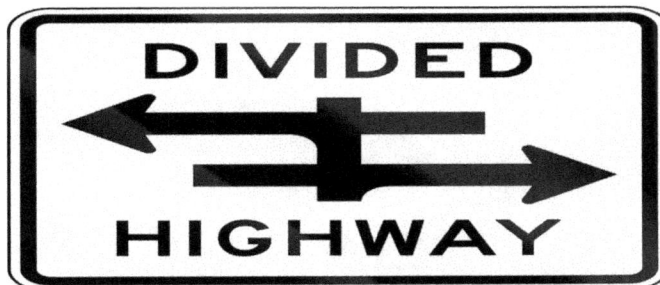

Acceptance is the last phase of grieving your divorce. For some, this means calling a ceasefire and being civil to one another after a long battle. For others, it means combined holidays and vacations. In both cases, there is a peaceful resignation that the marriage could not sustain and that a split was unavoidable.

When you reconcile that you will both be happier apart, the decision has been made. Preparing for what comes next consists of understanding the stages in the grief cycle. Acknowledging you will experience them at various times helps to alleviate some of the fear associated with the unknown. You will grieve and then you will be okay.

SECTION FIVE

What Is a Good Divorce?

SECTION FIVE

What is a Good Divorce?

List ten things a good divorce means to you:

1) _____

2) _____

3) _____

4) _____

5) _____

6) _____

7) _____

8) _____

9) _____

10) _____

DROP THE BITTERNESS

Divorce is imminent. You have decided your relationship is never going to work and there is no going back. You have analyzed every aspect of your marriage and your contribution to its demise. You have gone through the stages of grief, experiencing many of them repeatedly. You are tired of discussing it, crying over it, and being frustrated by it. The feeling of being shrouded in misery one more day seems unbearable, and moving on means survival.

Think of it this way. Your car is inoperable. When you take it to a mechanic to determine the problem, they tell you that you need a new engine. After weighing your options, you choose to replace the vehicle rather than replace one part at a time. It's too costly and difficult to repair. Your former vehicle provided a lot of good times and interesting adventures; however, it has become a struggle to maintain and operate.

Do you:

- Take a hammer to your old ride because it isn't what it used to be?
- Accuse the car of being a lemon?
- Get frustrated and yell at the mechanic who delivered the bad news?
- Blame the dealer who sold you the car in the first place?
- Rip up every photo you had of the car?
- Refuse to associate with anyone who has a similar car?
- Stop talking to individuals who rode in that car?
- Decide on alternate transportation because all cars are bad?

Chances are that you accept your losses and move on. Why is it so hard to do the same with our relationships? What seems irrational or absurd to do with a car we no longer drive is exactly what many do to their exes when divorcing.

Try to depersonalize and neutralize your sense of rejection. Simply because you or your partner decided you weren't good together doesn't mean either of you are bad people. You may both be good individuals who acted inappropriately when your relationship became challenging. If you were to video some of your interactions, you would be surprised by the behavior. The words that were spoken, the look on your faces, the tone in your voices. Both of you became unattractive in your frustration. Partners don't reject each other as much as they reject the behavior of someone in an unhappy marriage.

Own your behavior. If you have examined your relationship and what went wrong, chances are you have a good grasp on the mistakes you made in the marriage. If not, a counselor can help with this. Once you admit your faults, a heartfelt apology comes easier. Acknowledging you had areas of weakness and regret disarms your partner in most cases.

Recognize your partner for the good in them and stop shaming them for their liabilities. Even if they acted selfishly or irresponsibly, that is their problem and not yours. A friend of mine complained her husband was domineering and controlling and blamed him for ruining their marriage. However, he was exactly that way when they were dating. He veiled it by being a bit more tolerant and romantic, but it was always there underneath the hearts and flowers. In essence, she was discrediting him for being himself.

As I mentioned previously, my ex-husband is an introvert. He internalized his thoughts and preferred to work through his problems alone. Having a low tolerance for conflict, he kept things from me if he thought it might upset me. His privacy and need to process information internally made him appear withdrawn and unavailable. I labeled him cold when, in reality, he had always possessed those traits. The only difference was that early on in the relationship they weren't so pronounced as he worked around them to get to me. As the relationship evolved, he fell back into his old pattern of behaving. Rather than pull out all of the stops to meet my emotional needs, he slipped back into his comfort zone. It alienated us further when I criticized his personality. It was wrong of me to disparage who he was because I felt disconnected from him.

Be compassionate toward your partner. The pain and hurt you are undergoing is something they are experiencing as well. Though one partner may want the divorce more than the other, both individuals are suffering a tremendous disintegration. The loss of the dream you both shared is significant. The loss of friends, in-laws, residences, money, and the unification of a family system is overwhelming for both. The emotional and physical damages from divorce are substantial, and rebuilding will take time. Individuals tally up their losses and fail to acknowledge all their partner sacrificed as well.

It amazes me how two people fall in love, have children, build a home and a life together, only to become mortal enemies. So focused on hating their ex-partner and remaining bitter because things didn't turn out as planned, they perpetuate the fight. Both forget they wouldn't have those things without the other. If they could reframe the situation to be grateful for what the other person provided when things were good, it would make for a better divorce.

Divorce is not a terminal illness. Nor is it a death sentence. It is not the end of all that was before it. It is a transition. Perhaps it is a situation you didn't initiate; however, it doesn't help to drag around your cross-to-bear so others take pity upon you. Being the victim gets old. Friends will rally around you early on to promote your positive mental health. As you persist in your effort to feel sorry for yourself, they will fall by the wayside. Good friends build you up and make you stronger, as opposed to pitying you while you stay stuck in the past.

Playing the victim will backfire by keeping you in a destructive frame of mind. Associates begin to question your mental stability when all you manage to discuss is how horrible your ex was and how unfair life is now. It is impossible to get to a better place when you remain undesirable and unpleasant. No one wants to be subjected to negativity repeatedly. It becomes maddening. Good or bad, relationships change as we change. They get better or they get worse. Few remain the same. Your relationship ended, now move on. Chances are that you will discover new possibilities when you become positive and open to embracing it.

FACE YOUR FEARS

Do not let fear consume and overwhelm you. Divorce is doable. As horrible as it may seem, it can be managed.

In life, it is not about the bad things that happen to you, it is about how you react to the bad things that happen. You cannot control how and when the next disaster will strike. However, you can be as prepared as possible by building on your resources.

By resources, I refer to your emotional, economical, and professional assets. The emotional connections are your family and friends who offer support in your time of need. Economical relates to the assets and savings you have accumulated over the years. The professional considerations involve your preparedness for a career and your contacts in the workplace.

Though my father was old school in assuming I would become a wife and mother, he insisted I complete a college degree in the event I needed "something to fall back on." He knew better than anyone that the best laid plans can be derailed unexpectedly.

Along those lines, "We make plans and God laughs." Life is unpredictable and it is advisable to plan for the best and prepare for the worst. It does no good to complain and whine about how it should or could have been. Life is volatile and, by developing resources to deal with it, you strengthen your capabilities.

It's never too late to join a support group or network with others who are experiencing similar hardships. There is always time to go back to school, learn a new trade, or get a job. It may seem impossible when your energy is low and emotions are high. However, it can be done and even liberating.

Fear is the enemy, not your partner. That understanding is critical before being able to get a good divorce. Your partner is not responsible for managing your fears and insecurities. You are never guaranteed your spouse will always be there for you. They may get physically injured, become seriously ill, or suddenly die. You should equip yourself to handle the unforeseen and not place all of your expectations for happiness squarely on your partner.

List your top five fears about divorce:

1) _____

2) _____

3) _____

4) _____

5) _____

Most divorcées will tell you they worry about their children, money (finances and employment), the stigma of divorce (what other people think), loneliness, and making a mistake by leaving. If you have done all you can to save your marriage and have not acted in haste, you will feel more grounded in your decision. Most importantly, you must acknowledge that all relationships end. Through either a divorce or a death, there will come a time when we must be prepared to go it alone.

Fear of Harming the Children

A former boss of mine repeated this saying often. "The speed of the leader is the speed of the gang."

Though he referred to himself and the workplace, it is true in families as well. Longitudinal studies regarding the impact of divorce on children vary. However, all concede that staying together in a toxic relationship for the sake of the children creates more damage than the actual divorce. The general consensus is that divorce isn't necessarily bad for children, depending on the circumstances. If the parents handle it with aplomb and grace, their offspring will reflect that sense of wellbeing.

A student of mine who was a single parent recalled a time when she was going through a financial hardship. She and her five-year-old daughter were preparing to have dinner when their apartment went dark. Once she realized she had forgotten to pay an overdue electric bill, she blocked her panic from rising. Not allowing her internal hysterics to surface, she made it a party. By not giving into her fears and frightening her child, she lit candles instead. As the responsible adult, she chose to turn calamity into an adventure. Rather than worry her daughter unnecessarily, she decided to have fun with it until she could pay the bill the next day.

The same example should be applied for parents undergoing a divorce. Simply because they suffer the negative effects of it, they don't need to impose those feelings and fears on their children.

The beauty of children is that they are extremely resilient and adaptable. Initially children report being anxious and confused by divorce. It is imperative for couples to put aside their ongoing feud and focus on making their children feel loved and secure.

Unfortunately, the partner who perceives themselves as the wronged party frequently vents to those closest to them. Craving attention and sympathy while feeling a sense of injustice, they play to their audience, often their children. While in this mindset, the individual does more harm than good. They make the mistake of:

- Including the children in adult conversations that are inappropriate for their developmental level
- Being critical and speaking negatively about the other parent
- Acting out emotionally in front of the children, making them fearful
- Sharing too much information with the children to gain their support
- Using the children as hostages to hurt the other parent
- Trying to buy their children's love through extravagant gifts or vacations
- Creating drama to satisfy their victim mentality, causing chaos in the household
- Dividing the household and alienating the other parent out of spite
- Forcing the children to choose sides
- Allowing the children to use the divorce as an excuse for bad behavior

- Serving as a bad example on how to cope with disappointment and loss

Individuals who focus entirely on themselves during the divorce act irrationally. I have seen men so infuriated about the divorce that they leave the state and the country. By withholding emotional, physical, and financial support, they feel vindicated at the risk of harming their children.

I have also witnessed the opposite with a man who left his wife after years of unhappiness. Weary of the constant battling and unsuccessful trips to marriage counselors, he made a conscious decision to leave a difficult situation. He believed that by remaining in a caustic relationship, he set a poor example for his girls. Making certain his children would remain in the house they were raised in and attend the same schools, he sought stability for them. He bought a home close to them so they could visit whenever they wanted.

However, his attempts to make the transition as peaceful as possible for his children were met with sabotage from his ex. She undermined him in every way possible for years to follow. The children matured and, though saddened by her antics, eventually acknowledged, "You know how she is…"

Exes spend an inordinate amount of negative energy to prove they were right and the other parent was wrong. This has a way of backfiring and making the injured party look crazy. Who in their right mind would spend endless hours causing their children to suffer the ills of their parents? Couples fight to give and get the best for their children. However, when exes act selfishly, willfully damaging their children's relationship with the other parent, it becomes pathological.

Once couples put aside their differences and act like responsible adults who are concerned about the welfare of their children, the children will benefit. It is the parents' job to comfort the children, not the other way around. If the children perceive discord, they will feel uneasy and worry about the future. If they experience harmony and a united approach to making certain their needs are met, they will feel more secure and confident.

It is up to the parents to set the tone for their children's new reality. It can be a series of harmonious events or it can be a long string of contentious interactions. The children will follow the lead of the parents, good or bad. It is that simple.

Fear of not having enough money

With divorce so prevalent in our society, the courts have standards as to the financial division and obligation of the divorced couple. This varies from state to state, especially regarding alimony. The rule of thumb is a 50/50 split of assets and a set amount for child support based on the number of children until the children reach the age of eighteen.

Though the guidelines are fairly straightforward, couples continue to spend large sums of money battling each other with lawyers who promise to get them more than their fair share. I am aware of couples who have spent over a hundred thousand dollars to get exactly what they would have gotten without the legal battle.

When it comes to the division of assets, the court isn't concerned about assuming the role of moral authority. They aren't going to weigh in on who was right and who was wrong, and there is no reward or punishment for being either. Whether individuals have had affairs, gambling problems, or expensive spending habits, the formula for a financial settlement is fairly standardized.

Couples invariably fight over money. Though it makes sense to divide all assets and financial accounts equally, there are residual emotions associated with spending.

- The injustice they feel regarding the divorce is transferred to the finances.
- It is now the only thing they can control about the relationship.
- It is often used as a weapon against their partner.
- They react out of fear as their lifestyle is compromised and their future survival is threatened.
- They are angry about having to share the possessions they have accumulated over time.
- They are angry about having to go back to work if they were a stay-at-home parent.
- It is a symbol to outsiders about who won and who lost in the divorce.
- Money carries power and influence in the marriage as well as the divorce.

Money is a contributing factor as to why couples find it so difficult to get a good divorce. Often times people tend to think of a divorce as being successful if the monetary rewards from it are great. This line of thinking is skewed. When people fight for the lion's share of the money, it creates an antagonistic environment that perpetuates anger and dislike.

Divorce is costly. It isn't just the division of assets one must consider, but also you will have double the expenses from then on. Living apart means two residences and all the outlays associated with both. Couples divide their resources and double their living expenses. Separately, you both have less after the divorce than you did before.

Dealing with these facts can create an atmosphere of resentment, or it can be a fair and positive foundation from which you both move forward. You can choose to fight about money and complain you have less, or you can accept your new reality and help each other to recover.

Regarding money, it is far better to insure both parties get their fair share. There are those individuals who feel it is never enough. However, happiness and peace of mind do not have price tags. Each of you lost money and gained freedom.

I recall a mediator stating to a client of mine that he needed to give up one more monetary reward to his ex before negotiations were completed. My client asked why, since he felt he had been stretched enough. She told him if he wanted the divorce to be finalized that day, then he would have to pay for it. She called it the bitch tax. If he wanted to be rid of his ex and conclude the settlement, he needed to offer up one more financial reward.

The best financial solution is one where both parties remain friendly and demonstrate genuine concern for each other. Due to the economy, my losing my business, and my ex being laid off, we both suffered terrible financial blows. It took each of us years to recover from the aftershock. We went into our separation with a good deal of assets to divide, only to discover we had far less at the time of our divorce.

The series of unfortunate circumstances helped unite us in our efforts to make sure the other person had the capital they needed to move forward. We didn't blame each other, nor did we try to take advantage of the other. Perhaps that is why we were both so generous, because we had lost so much.

Components of a good financial settlement are the following:

• Be realistic. Don't expect to come out financially ahead in the divorce.

• A 50/50 split of assets

• A 50/50 split of savings

• Be generous regarding sentimental items. Let go of your partner's and you will most likely be able to retain yours. Goodwill is the most important tool for an equitable agreement.

• Avoid lawyers who encourage you to go for more. That typically means more money for them and less for you. What is the cost of an amicable divorce versus a contentious one?

• If one person has been the breadwinner, allow for the other to receive additional compensation until they are able to function independently. Expectations and guidelines should be made clear at the time of the divorce to avoid it dragging out.

• Understand that though you married this person and shared a life, they are no longer responsible for you financially. You are your best asset and need to develop ways to support yourself.

Money is the best way to keep two individuals engaged in combat regarding what should have been. What they sacrificed for each other muddies the waters of their financial stream. They believe if they get more money, it will make things better. It doesn't. Only a change of attitude and a sense of self-sufficiency will make up for what they lost.

I relocated across the country several times for my husband's professional advancement. The cost to me was leaving my family, friends, jobs, and houses I loved. When we divorced, I used this against him, complaining that, while we focused on building his career, we sacrificed mine.

In retrospect, our mutual goal of developing his career was a choice we had both made. It afforded me a good lifestyle, an opportunity to live in some of the most beautiful places in the U.S., and interesting opportunities. The journey was great for a while, though we eventually decided on different destinations.

The fact is, we built our marriage together and both suffered when it dissolved. Neither one more than the other. We wouldn't have what we did without the other, and we both deserve a part of it in the end. The idea of punishing my ex because things didn't work out as planned is absurd. He experienced as much pain, uncertainty, and loss as I did. No amount of money is going to change that.

What brings comfort is that we remain friends. I wish the best for him and his new life and want him to acquire success where we failed. Just as I intend to pursue my dreams as before. It is up to the individual to cut their losses and rebuild. What we had as a couple is gone, except for the mutual respect that remains.

Fear of Dealing with the Stigma of Divorce

Though the stigma of divorce isn't what it used to be, it is, at the very least, embarrassing. Couples have a difficult time admitting they failed. Individuals have problems conceding their part in it and have a tendency to blame their partner for their disastrous relationship. While pointing fingers at each other (sometimes the middle one), couples end the relationship under the pretense that I am good person, however my partner is not.

Self-esteem is at the root of feeling stigmatized by the divorce. Couples tend to feel "less than" while experiencing divorce. Adapting to all of the changes challenges their stability in a way that is overwhelming at times. Most likely friends and family have seen signs that all is not well in paradise. However, it remains uncomfortable to tell their doctor, dentist, co-workers, children's teachers, and other associates in their lives. It hurts to lose.

Dr. Phil McGraw has stated that what other people think of you is none of your business.

This is particularly true when experiencing a divorce. Reframe what is happening to you in a way that empowers you. Rather than focus on being a loser for getting a divorce, congratulate yourself for being brave enough to get out of a bad situation. There are numerous couples who stay in unsatisfying relationships because of fear.

You are a warrior to do what is best for you and your family, regardless if it is an unpopular decision. People will judge you. That is their problem, not yours.

Confidence begins with knowing you are doing the right thing. When you accept this, rest easy. Wallowing in guilt, shame, and doubt will not help you mend. Don't give other people the power to prevent you from doing what your heart requires. Trying to save face or maintain a front is exhausting and eventually works against you. It is frustrating for couples who can't stand to be around each other, yet do so at other people's insistence.

Building your self-worth is essential to recovering from the divorce. Things that will help elevate your self-esteem are the following:

• When things become overwhelming, fake it to make it. Acting self-assured will boost your confidence. Head up, shoulders back. Walk like a winner even when you feel like a loser.

• Know who you are. Focus and build on your strengths. You have time to correct your weaknesses. Now is when you need your powers to propel you forward. Don't allow others to create doubt in your mind. Only you know where you have been and where you want to go. Don't let outsiders interfere with your path.

• Surround yourself with good people. Not people who tell you what you want to hear. Rather, people who will listen, lift you up, and encourage you to be strong. Those who have experienced a divorce are helpful because they know what you are going through. It builds assurance in knowing they survived.

• Think and speak positively. Don't speak poorly about your ex in public and don't complain about your life then or now. See the good around you and more will follow. Our thoughts become our actions, so make them positive. Destructive thoughts and actions produce negativity that is unattractive and detrimental to your recovery.

• Call on your beliefs. Whatever belief system you adopt should be enlisted for insight. Whether it is religion, astrology, psychology, or any body of knowledge that provides comfort, seek it out. Divine intervention is most welcome when feeling helpless or alone. Inspirational reading helps to fortify your inner core and keep fear at bay.

• Value yourself. Take stock of your accomplishments and successes. Don't let others criticize your decisions or minimize your achievements. If they make you feel bad for not living their life or their lie, ignore them. What is important is that you don't buy into their self-righteous attitude in order to be accepted. Live your own truth. You don't owe anyone an explanation. Know your worth and do not let others tell you otherwise.

Fear of Loneliness

At the end of a relationship, there may be separation anxiety related to loneliness. Three contributors to loneliness are:

- Fear and doubt of not being able to find a fulfilling relationship
- Negative feelings about being rejected
- Low self-esteem.

Loneliness should not be confused with being alone. Feeling lonely may still be present in social settings. The loneliness typically experienced during or after a divorce is situational. The disruption in family life has affected all of the relationships associated with it.

Cognitive-oriented therapies are helpful to combat the feeling of being lonesome through modifying irrational beliefs and self-defeating patterns. When individuals experience lack of control over their lives, they tend to become anxious and frustrated leading to complications in their social relationships.

Steps to overcoming loneliness:

Understand it is temporary. You are adjusting to your new social setting. Being alone in the house without your ex and the children takes getting used to, as does cooking for one and eating alone.

Fill your alone time with activities that help you grow. Read self-help books that sort out childhood issues, improves self-esteem, or provides insights into relationships. Inspire yourself regularly.

Engage in anxiety-reducing activities. Classes in exercise and yoga, knitting, watching movies, reading, or getting pedicures are all useful ways to combat angst.

Develop a social network of individuals who understand what you are going through and will support your recovery. Tell them what you need. If it is difficult to be alone on Sundays, arrange for a group to attend church and go to brunch together.

Explore new career opportunities that will introduce you to fresh ideas and a diverse group of people. Expand your network and occasions to meet new individuals.

Develop new interests. I tell the recently divorced individuals to cultivate hobbies or activities that will attract the kind of people they want to meet. If you enjoy tennis, join a club and interact with people who play the game. Go to a driving range and work on your swing if you want to meet golfers. Conversely, if you have a problem with social drinking, stay away from bars and clubs.

Get out and about. Don't isolate yourself. Your next partner will most likely not come knocking on your door. Hiding behind four walls and your children will not alleviate your feelings of loneliness, it will only add to it.

Keep a journal of your feelings and document your progress. Healing happens at a slow and gradual pace. Though it may feel as though not much has changed, when you read where you were a year ago, you will be astonished at how far you have come.

Reflect on the past and what went wrong to design a better future. Focusing on being proactive and productive takes the sting away from the loneliness that you are feeling in the moment.

Breathe. Don't allow the fear and loneliness to choke the daylight out of you.

Fear of Having Made a Mistake

It is normal to question if you made a mistake, especially when you face the adverse aspects associated with divorce. The losses are real, the fears are haunting, and the decision is agonizing. No one can predict the future.

If your approach to the divorce was methodical, well thought out, and nonreactive, then don't look back. Be present in the moment, prepare for a better tomorrow, and trust your heart. Develop a road map, ask for directions, and most of all enjoy the ride. For additional reassurance consider the following:

- Acknowledge your marriage is over. Live in the present, not in the past.
- Accept what it cost you emotionally, physically, and financially. Begin to rebuild.
- Recall why you wanted the divorce and that it was inevitable. Remember, things look better from a distance, and we have a way of remembering the good and forgetting the bad.
- Draw on your reserves and rely on them to carry you. This too shall pass.
- Let go of guilt and regret. It happened for a reason.
- Visualize what the future looks. No one and nothing is holding you back. It's up to you.
- Transition from anger to forgiveness, from depression to happiness, and from the past to the future.

A comforting thought is that unlike death, divorce is reversible. If you believe it was truly a mistake and discover that your partner feels the same way, go back. A fair number of couples have reconciled and do better the second time around. In some cases, there is the possibility of rekindling the flame and starting over together.

What is important is that you determined what your bottom line was and acted upon it. There is no crystal ball. The decision you made to divorce was a culmination of your past experiences, your current knowledge, and your future desires. Assuming you initiated it out of necessity, sought answers instead of revenge, and worked hard to understand the situation rather than blame your partner, you did the right thing.

Only time will tell if the divorce was best for all concerned.

Everyone does the best they can in the moment. Treat yourself and your partner respectfully, and the rest will fall into place. There will be times when you second-guess yourself, your ex, and the divorce. Let the process develop naturally. Forcing issues and attempting to control all variables won't work. Trust the universe and yourself.

MANAGE YOUR STRESS

Stress is part of life. It is multiplied during a divorce. Couples go into survival mode and everything is a threat to their equilibrium. They face injustices that make them angry and afraid. "Resentment comes from anger, just as smoke comes from fire."

While in this destructive cycle, couples experience tremendous frustration that creates anxiety and irrational thinking. The feelings compound each other in a vicious cycle with stress as a result.

Ways to manage stress:

Put yourself first. Look after yourself and make time for you. Take care of yourself, especially at a time when others depend on you. Your children, boss, and family need you to be strong, healthy and intact. If you ignore your physical and emotional needs, you are placing yourself and those you love at risk.

Meditate. Whether you engage in contemplation or actual meditation, take time out to reflect. Look within and listen to the quiet. Pray for wisdom and a way out of the darkness. Relax and let your spirit rise to the occasion. Healing begins from within.

Work out. Exercise however you desire. Dance, take a spin class, play tennis, run, or do aerobics. Burn off the frustration in a positive way. Get your heart rate up, sweat, and push through your exhaustion.

Learn to say no. Others may demand things you can no longer provide. Drop the committee if it's too much work and not enough reward. Teach your children to self-amuse if you need a little down time. It's not advantageous to surround yourself with needy people as your limited reserves run low.

Learn how to relax. Deep breathing, hot baths, massages, a good book, yoga, long walks, listening to music, or a much needed a glass of wine helps. Whatever it takes to calm you should be repeated frequently (aside from the wine). Divorce is a beat down. Being able to relax is key to centering yourself and regrouping.

Embrace the new. Change is not your enemy. Now is the time to lose ten pounds, color or cut your hair. Shake it up! Try on the new you for size. Buy a new piece of furniture or art for your place. Let go of the items and reminders that make you sad. Cleanse in a fresh future.

Laugh. At a time like this, humor is your best ally. Divorce is troubling but it has its amusing moments. I recall a time when my former boyfriend's ex was a nightmare. The name calling, constant drama, and craziness from her was alarming. Her antics were embarrassing and upsetting, to say the least. Given there was nothing we could do to change her bad behavior, we were forced to endure it. We decided to treat encounters with her like a Seinfeld episode as opposed to Judge Judy. Rather than demand rationality and justice, we found the comedy and absurdity in the situation. Her behavior didn't change, however our response to it did.

Reward yourself. Go out with friends, buy the dress, take a weekend away. It doesn't have to be all turmoil and work. Turn your face toward the sun and bask in the light. Applaud yourself for all you have accomplished.

LEARN TO FORGIVE

Forgiveness doesn't come easily. Similar to working through anger, forgiving someone who has wronged you takes determination and self-talk.

We forgive because we choose to do so. We may not feel like it and we may not want to do it. However, we make a choice to forgive for our sake. They may not deserve it, but we do. Holding onto anger and resentment does more damage to us than to the person it is directed towards. Forgiveness requires mindful attention and a will to let the past go. Living in hurt and resentment is not living. The choice is to be free of it and proceed in a positive manner.

Understand that life is fluid. It is ever changing and not always kind. Things happen that we would prefer didn't happen. We may not have control over certain events; however, we have control over how we react to them.

Just as life has been testing you, the same is true for your partner. Most likely, neither of you expected your marriage to end in divorce. Some steps to forgiveness are as follows:

Letting go is vital. Release the anger, resentment, bitterness and blame. It may sound impossible to do. It is not. Soul-searching creates self-awareness. This in turn results in ownership of what you did wrong and a willingness to share the blame. When faulting your partner is no longer feasible, empathy and understanding follow.

Perspective-taking is a must. When you understand your partner's point of view, it helps clarify their behavior. Did they hurt you because they were insecure? Did they do it out of jealousy and envy? How were they suffering? Instead of demonizing them, try to identify with them. You don't have to rescue them or excuse their wrongdoings while attempting to understand them.

Eliminate all the "ifs." My father used to quote, "If ifs were camels, beggars would ride." If he was more affectionate… if he stopped drinking… if she lost weight… if she was less controlling. This longing of "what ifs" changes nothing. It keeps you stuck regretting and obsessing over what could have been. Focus on what you have and not what you don't have.

Accept the reality and finality of the divorce. Wanting a "do over" or wishing you had never gone down that path is futile. Your emphasis should be on the lessons you learned and the gifts you received. The truth is, you both contributed to the marriage as well as the divorce. Perhaps you weren't a good match in the first place and are better off without each other. That admission alone fosters forgiveness. You may have been good together at one point in time. Since that is no longer the case, move past it.

Compassion is necessary. No one goes through a divorce without feeling pain. Even if you believe you are the injured party, you both sacrificed something. For the man, it may be money and not being with his children as often as he would like. For the woman, it may be financial security and the stability of an intact family. Everyone gives up something, no matter how it appears from the outside.

Revenge is not restitution. It's been said that happiness is the best revenge. Nothing is more attractive and enviable than happiness. When partners are vengeful or spiteful, it not only makes them look bad, it also keeps everyone locked in a vicious cycle of crazy. The negative energy spent in payback and retribution does more harm to the person doing it. It isn't worth the fight.

Eliminate further expectations regarding your ex. Nothing infuriates as much as unmet expectations. Most likely, one reason you are no longer together is that you felt your partner had let you down. Accept that you cannot change this person or how they behave. When they react to a situation in a manner that used to drive you crazy, detach. Allow them to be themselves without criticism. It isn't your problem. Remain neutral and unemotional. Laugh about it and be grateful it is no longer your concern.

Look long-term, not short-term. You may still feel the sting of your divorce and unrealized dreams. Know that these feelings will weaken over time. As you go on to live your life, the goal should be coming to peace with your situation. When children are involved, there will be graduations, weddings, and events that include you both. How great if both parents can attend as friends with smiling faces. Future celebrations or funerals should be filled with a quiet acceptance of what was and what is.

Embrace a spirit of cooperation. Becoming friends may be a stretch. Respectful acquaintances is a start. Life is tough. Under the threat of the multitude of things that could go wrong, we all need support from one another. Two people who once shared a love and life together—not to mention children—should have each other's interest at heart. Though no longer a priority, it should remain a factor. In the end, treating your ex as you would like to be treated is a good thing.

Encourage your spouse to do better. Applaud when they move on. Let them know you wish the best for them and hope they find their happy ever after. A client spoke so viciously of his ex that I asked him to list three things he once loved about her. Seeing he was stumped, I suggested a few that got him thinking and remembering. Feelings change, as do people, and that is why divorce is so prevalent. However, if we are able to recall what we felt at a different time, it helps to lessen the contemptuous feelings toward our ex in the present.

TRANSCEND THE DIVORCE

Do not let divorce define you. It is now part of you, like the color of your eyes or where you were born. "D" is not the scarlet letter and you don't have to wear the shame of it on your lapel.

I recall a time when I went out to dinner with my immediate family. Feeling depressed and ashamed over my divorce, my father put his arm around me. He assured me his successful marriage was as much luck as it was hard work.

NO
EXIT

Don't beat yourself up too much about your marital failure. It doesn't matter if it's a result of bad luck, bad choices, bad timing, or bad judgment, you are the one left to deal with the consequences. It is just one small part of you.

When the relationship damages the two people in it and negatively affects the children, ending it is the best solution. Committing to a good divorce is the best option. The price of your mental and physical health is not worth having to endure abuse, chronic conflict, disrespect, or being in a loveless partnership. The collateral damage is minimized when you practice some of the tools and techniques outlined in this book.

A divorce is NOT:

A death sentence. No one has died from a divorce.

The end. It is the end of the relationship; however, it is a new beginning for the individuals who were in it.

A failure on your part. It is the situation that failed, not you. Take the guilt and shame associated with a disastrous relationship and turn them into a life lesson. It is a stepping stone to self-awareness and better relationships down the road.

A deficiency in you. Though childhood wounds may have contributed negatively to your adult relationships, we all come with baggage from our youth. Married, single, and divorced alike. Divorce doesn't mean you are "less than" anyone else. It doesn't signify there is something wrong with you.

Always a bad thing. There was a time when divorce was not a possibility. This was a time before women were college graduates, property owners, breadwinners, CEO's, and entrepreneurs. Women were entrapped in impossible relationships and forced to obey. Divorce is liberating if the relationship was unbearable.

A social stigma. At a time when divorce was rare, outsiders frowned upon the individuals who left a marriage as duds or damaged goods. Today, divorce is common and there is no dishonor in it, if it is handled properly.

A sign of weakness. On the contrary, divorce requires a lot of strength and determination. For those that follow the path of least resistance and require financial security at all cost, divorce is beyond their scope of possibility. It takes courage to give up your home, divide your assets, and venture out alone. With no guarantees for a new job, new love, and a happy life, sometimes it is easier to stay put.

Easy. When partners accuse the other of taking the easy way out by leaving the relationship, that is short-sighted. There is nothing easy about divorce. The emotional and financial demands are tremendous. Even good divorces are difficult.

The only option. I have heard people say divorce isn't an option, when in fact that is wishful thinking on their part. Divorce is always an option; it just isn't the only one. Separating for a period of time is a good alternative. Separation may mean taking time out from each other by residing in different places, or it can mean a legal split. My ex-husband and I legally separated for a period of years. Certain we would not reunite, we legally separated to end the marriage and in turn saved the relationship. He provided my healthcare benefits and I gave him tax reimbursements. We helped each transition to the divorce. It was the beginning of our good divorce.

Ideal. If any other chance is available for a successful relationship, divorce should be a last resort. It is costly and taxing in many ways on all of the parties involved. It takes its toll on everyone and remains complicated long after. Divorce requires a great deal of adjustment, maturity, and forgiveness.

DATING AFTER THE DIVORCE

The most important essentials in dating after divorce is to exercise caution, take it slow, and don't expose your children to all of your dates. Exploration of a suitable partner should remain your business alone and kept remote from the children. Don't include them until a friendship or relationship develops. Introducing them to every prospect is puzzling and unsettling.

Until you are ready take it to the next level, which involves bringing someone into your home and interacting with your children, keep it distant. Ten things to consider while dating are:

Who are you now after the divorce? Assess what you learned from your past relationship and the divorce. What things did you discover about yourself, good and bad? What aspects about you require change? Were you controlling, unappreciative, demanding, lazy, uncommunicative, unaffectionate, or preoccupied? What areas need improving before you enter into another relationship? Individual counseling helps to define your strengths as well as your weaknesses. Reading on the subject of relationships should be mandatory before entering into another one.

Be careful not to project unresolved issues with your ex onto your new partner. The more evolved couples are in their divorce, the better equipped they are to take on another relationship. The important point here is to limit any residual backlash from the previous partnership. Whatever problems existed in your marriage will be sensitive subjects in the new relationship. Because your former partner drank too much doesn't afford you the right to monitor your date's alcohol consumption. Your coping mechanisms in the old relationship shouldn't automatically transfer to the new one. Keep former problems with your ex in the past. Do not transpose them onto your new relationship.

Define what it is you want in a partner going forward. Don't date someone who is the opposite of your spouse just because they are nothing alike. You may be turned off by your ex due to the difficult marriage and divorce. However, people generally are drawn to a type because that kind of person suits them. You developed a serious long-term relationship with someone whom you believed was a good match for you. When things didn't work out, it doesn't necessitate that you should run in the opposite direction. If your husband was a salesman, it doesn't mean you should avoid all salesmen and date accountants. Be careful not to eliminate people based on categorizing them improperly and presuming they are like your ex.

Go slow. Even if you find someone intriguing immediately after the divorce, don't get serious straightaway. It is in your best interest to experience several dates and get a feel for what's out there. If you are meant to be with this person, they will be there after you have gotten back into the swing of things. You want to be certain the feelings you're experiencing for this person are genuine and are not generated from loneliness, insecurity, or fear. Men have complained to me that after a few dates with a divorcée, the woman pushed for a serious relationship. Men fear women want to latch onto them without even knowing them, solely because they want to be part of a couple.

A good place to start dating is online. It offers both choice and distance, something new divorcées require. Pressure from outsiders is minimized and privacy is respected. A meeting or date can be quick as a cup of coffee. There is more control and less risk regarding online dating. You choose a match based on a profile you find interesting and pursue it at your own pace. Additionally, online dating, if you are cautious, provides more options for divorcées than they had in the past. Another option is to attend any of the numerous organized events for singles. Matchmaking has become a big business to your benefit.

Brush up on dating do's and don'ts, especially if it's been a while. There are a lot of books that give great tips on dating at any stage and at any age. When you were younger, there were less variables to deal with. You had a larger pool of single partners to draw from. College campuses, massive apartment complexes catering to young professionals, urban areas with numerous restaurants and bars, and single friends to name a few. If you now live in the suburbs with children, your opportunities for meeting someone are diminished. Also, there is less baggage when couples are younger. It was an easier time to date before failed marriages, failed careers, children, debt, and disappointments.

Whether you are 20 or 80, men love the chase. Dating has evolved in many ways over the decades. However, one thing remains the same. If a man is into you, he will show it. He calls, invites you places, introduces you to his friends and family, and is interested in your life. He is attentive to you and your feelings while he can't keep his hands off of you. He asks to be with you more often, not less. Basically he can't get enough of you, no matter how busy he is with work. Simply because you have a career, manage a household, and are raising children, doesn't mean you should take charge with dating. Without a doubt, you are capable, but I recommend not going against nature. Just because you *can* doesn't mean you *should*. I often tell women to let the game come to them. Unfortunately, many young women force the issue by making themselves too available. Frequently men tell me when a woman is too obtainable, it is a red flag. They want to fight for the woman everyone wants. It's a story as old as time and it hasn't changed.

When you do fall in love again and feel you have found a suitable partner, examine every possible issue or scenario under a microscope. It is best to approach love with feelings from the heart and eyes wide open. It took me two years in a long distance relationship before I relocated to the state where I now reside with my new husband. We debated every issue to make certain we understood each other without reservation. I was concerned about raising his two young children. He made a spreadsheet as to the exact amount of time we would be spending with them, and we defined my role in their lives. We left nothing to the imagination regarding expectations. We made lists and outlines, then reviewed them and rewrote them. We discussed uncomfortable topics in advance. Though we were passionately in love, we forced ourselves to take a pen and highlight potential obstacles and pitfalls. We approached our relationship in an adult and realistic way.

Like it or not, handling the ex-spouse is part of the new relationship. It may take some trial and error to find the right equilibrium. It is most challenging when the ex feels wronged and hasn't gotten over it. Some make it a habit to sabotage their ex's new romance and interfere with their schedule. As ex's spar, the fallout impacts the new relationship. Anger and frustration are often unleashed on the undeserving. Projected negative emotions and bad moods make it problematic for everyone. Be patient. In most cases this, too, is temporary. Focus on civility and the future.

There is also the opposite scenario where one ex continues to accommodate the other to the point that it impedes their new relationship. Being too obliging may backfire when the new partner feels they constantly play second fiddle. Flexibility and balance are paramount. Pleasing the ex will not lessen the effects of the divorce;

it will only foster manipulation and interfere with new possibilities.

The same is true regarding children. I often tell people that no one will love your children to the same degree as you and your spouse. It isn't about DNA. It is about being there for the birth, their first words, steps, and significant milestones. The children will always be bonded with their parents in ways that cannot be denied. They possess a loyalty to them that step-parents must respect. Even when one parent acts crazy, children often stand by them, making excuses for bad behavior.

This is important to understand for two reasons. First, newcomers must respect this unique connection without question. Second, even though you love your children beyond measure, you cannot expect the same from your new partner. It will take time for them to develop a relationship with your children. Should you persist on making your children a priority in all instances and put their demands above everyone else's, you will lose the opportunity for a new relationship. Patience, tolerance, and most of all balance are mandatory when dealing with someone else's children in a relationship.

In conclusion, as undesirable and challenging as divorce is, it is a widespread reality. Though it should be circumvented whenever possible, sometimes it is unavoidable.

Before suffering a divorce, you should develop an understanding of what is involved. Divorce is rarely as easy and liberating as many falsely believe. Nor is it always wanted equally by both parties.

Though some exclaim that divorce is not an option when they walk down the aisle, it takes two to maintain that belief. If one person is unfulfilled and miserable, divorce is always a possibility.

We cannot control all of the variables in our relationship any more than we can control our partner. Because of this, we may find ourselves in an unsatisfying or toxic marriage that we are unable to manage. When issues have been exhausted, the counselors have given up, the children are being negatively affected, and the cloud of negativity cannot be lifted, divorce is a reasonable option.

A Fork in the Road, Your Guide to a Good Divorce, is for those considering divorce as well as for those who are in the midst of one. It does not encourage or endorse it as much as it acknowledges the reality of the split. By examining the emotions associated with divorce and promoting an understanding of the issues and their source, it focuses on scrutinizing problematic relationships.

Once the divorce has been initiated, *A Fork in the Road* illustrates the process of grief and recovery. Coping strategies and possible outcomes are explored for a better tomorrow. It provides an alternative to the stereotypical nasty divorce by suggesting that orchestrating the end of a marriage doesn't have to be ugly and contentious.

Because two people shared a life and then decided to travel in different directions doesn't have to mean the destruction of them both. Good people get divorced. The process doesn't have demonize them or turn them into mortal enemies. The alternative is developing the resources and knowledge to choose the good divorce.

About the Author

Gale D. Stanton has studied and worked in mental health and wellness for over three decades. She holds a Master of Arts degree in Counseling from Oakland University, Rochester Hills, Michigan, and has worked as a registered occupational therapist in psychiatric hospitals in Michigan and Florida. She became a pediatric therapy specialist for California Children Services prior to becoming a program director for a private college in San Diego, California, where she taught classes in Life-Span Development and Psychosocial Functioning. As an educator and program director, she developed an Occupational Therapy Assistant program accredited by the Accreditation Council of Occupational Therapy Education.

Ms. Stanton has both personal and professional experience with marriage and divorce. Urged by female clients and associates to create a relationship book that men would actually read, she developed *Two for the Road*, published in 2016. Written in a manual format that appeals to men, the relationship principles in the book are universal to both sexes. She designed this unique relationship guide to get the conversation started between couples. *Two for the Road* includes content and interactive exercises that promote constructive dialogues instead of one-sided monologues.

A Fork in the Road is her second book about relationships and marriage.

Raised in the suburb Bloomfield Hills, Michigan, outside of Detroit (the "Motor City"), she currently resides in a suburb of Dallas, Texas. As a trained therapist and educator, she has several other books underway that span the life stages of intimate relationships.

Gale D. Stanton
MA, OTR/L